255

World Bank Discussion Papers

Violence Against Women

The Hidden Health Burden

Lori L. Heise
with Jacquelin
and Adrienne

The World Bank
Washington, D.C.

Discussion Papers present results of country analysis or research that are circulated to encourage discussion and comment within the development community. To present these results with the least possible delay, the typescript of this paper has not been prepared in accordance with the procedures appropriate to formal printed texts, and the World Bank accepts no responsibility for errors. Some sources cited in this paper may be informal documents that are not readily available.

The findings, interpretations, and conclusions expressed in this paper are entirely those of the author(s) and should not be attributed in any manner to the World Bank, to its affiliated organizations, or to members of its Board of Executive Directors or the countries they represent. The World Bank does not guarantee the accuracy of the data included in this publication and accepts no responsibility whatsoever for any consequence of their use. The boundaries, colors, denominations, and other information shown on any map in this volume do not imply on the part of the World Bank Group any judgment on the legal status of any territory or the endorsement or acceptance of such boundaries.

The complete backlist of publications from the World Bank is shown in the annual *Index of Publications,* which contains an alphabetical title list (with full ordering information) and indexes of subjects, authors, and countries and regions. The latest edition is available free of charge from the Distribution Unit, Office of the Publisher, The World Bank, 1818 H Street, N.W., Washington, D.C. 20433, U.S.A., or from Publications, The World Bank, 66, avenue d'Iéna, 75116 Paris, France.

ISSN: 0259-210X

Lori L. Heise is director of the Violence, Health and Development Project, Pacific Institute for Women's Health, Washington, D.C. Jacqueline Pitanguy is president and founder of CEPIA (Citizenship, Studies, Information and Action), Rio de Janeiro, Brazil. Adrienne Germain is vice president of the International Women's Health Coalition, New York. At the time of writing, all were consultants to the World Bank's Population, Health and Nutrition Department.

Library of Congress Cataloging-in-Publication Data

Heisi, Lori.
      Violence against women : the hidden health burden / Lori L. Heise
  with Jacqueline Pitanguy and Adrienne Germain.
        p.   cm. — (World Bank discussion papers ; 255)
     Includes bibliographical references (p.   ).
     ISBN 0-8213-2980-4
     1. Wife abuse — Health aspects. 2. Women — Crimes against — Health
  aspects. 3. Sex crimes — Health aspects.   I. Pitanguy, Jacqueline.
  II. Germain, Adrienne.   III. International Bank for Reconstruction
  and Development.   IV. Title.   V. Series.
  HV6626.H38   1994
  362.1'968582200973 — dc20
                                     94-27745
                                        CIP

"Wife beating is an accepted custom...we are wasting our time debating the issue."

Comment made by parliamentarian during floor debates
on wife battering in Papua New Guinea
("Wife Beating," 1987).

"A wife married is like a pony bought; I'll ride her and whip her as I like."

Chinese proverb (Croll 1980).

"Women should wear *purdah* [head-to-toe covering] to ensure that innocent men do not get unnecessarily excited by women's bodies and are not unconsciously forced into becoming rapists. If women do not want to fall prey to such men, they should take the necessary precautions instead of forever blaming the men."

Comment made by a parliamentarian of the ruling Barisan National Party
during floor debates on reform of rape laws in Malaysia (Heise 1991).

"The boys never meant any harm to the girls. They just wanted to rape."

Statement by the deputy principal of St. Kizito's boarding school in Kenya
after 71 girls were raped and 19 others died in an attack by boys in the school
ascribed to the girls' refusal to join them in a strike
against the school's headmaster (Perlez 1991).

Breast bruised, brains battered,
Skin scarred, soul shattered,
Can't scream—neighbors stare,
Cry for help—no one's there.

    Stanza from a poem by Nenna Nehru, a battered Indian woman (APDC 1989).

"The child was sexually aggressive."

Justification given by a judge in British Columbia, Canada,
for suspending the sentence of a 33-year-old man who had
sexually assaulted a three-year-old girl
(Canada, House of Commons 1991).

"Are you a virgin? If you are not a virgin, why do you complain? This is normal."

Response by the assistant to the public prosecutor in Peru
when nursing student Betty Fernandez reported being sexually molested
by police officers while in custody (Kirk 1993).

Contents

Appendixes

Notes

Bibliography

Tables

Boxes

Foreword

Violence against women has recently been acknowledged as a human rights concern with a profound impact on the physical and mental well-being of those affected by it, but it has received little attention as a public health issue. The World Bank recognizes that much more needs to be known about the health consequences of gender violence, as well as their broader socioeconomic effects on development. This paper pulls together all the information available on the scope of the problem and the lessons to be learned from developing countries regarding how violence can be addressed through programmatic interventions.

This paper was prepared to raise awareness of the extent and consequences of violence against women. It also examines the implications of gender violence for health and development and suggests practical steps that can be taken toward eliminating violence against women. Although this paper is directed toward the health sector, strategies that can be taken in other sectors are also discussed. The primary audience of the paper is the staff of the World Bank, but we hope the paper will also benefit the design and implementation of health programs of other international agencies, governments, and nongovernmental organizations. This paper is one in a series of papers related to the broader issues affecting women's health.

Janet de Merode
Director
Population, Health and Nutrition Department
Human Resources Development and Operations Policy

Acknowledgments

The authors would like to thank the following people for their help in preparing and reviewing this document: Jacquelyn Campbell, Elizabeth Shrader Cox, Lea Guido, Simone Grilo Dinez, Kirrin Gill, Rita Raj Hashim, Emmanuel Jimenez, Mary Koss, JoAnne Leslie, Lisa Morris, Helen Saxenien, and Anne Tinker.

Abstract

Gender-based violence—including rape, domestic violence, mutilation, murder, and sexual abuse—is a profound health problem for women across the globe. Although gender violence is a significant cause of female morbidity and mortality, it is almost never seen as a public health issue. Recent World Bank estimates of the global burden of disease indicate that in established market economies gender-based victimization is responsible for one out of every five healthy days of life lost to women of reproductive age. On a per capita basis, the health burden imposed by rape and domestic violence in the industrial and developing world is roughly equivalent, but because the total disease burden is so much greater in the developing world, the percentage attributable to gender-based victimization is smaller. Nonetheless, on a global basis, the health burden from gender-based victimization is comparable to that from other conditions already high on the world agenda.

Female-focused violence also represents a hidden obstacle to economic and social development. By sapping women's energy, undermining their confidence, and compromising their health, gender violence deprives society of women's full participation. As the United Nations Fund for Women (UNIFEM) recently observed, "Women cannot lend their labor or creative ideas fully if they are burdened with the physical and psychological scars of abuse" (Carillo 1992, p.11).

This paper draws together existing data on the dimensions of violence against women worldwide and reviews available literature on the health consequences of abuse. It also explores the relationship between violence and other pressing issues, such as maternal mortality, health care utilization, child survival, AIDS prevention, and socioeconomic development.

To assist policymakers in addressing this issue, the paper explores interventions in primary prevention, justice system reform, health care response, programs to assist victims, and treatment and reeducation programs for perpetrators. It argues that any strategy to combat violence must attack the root causes of the problem in addition to treating its symptoms. This means challenging the social attitudes and beliefs that undergird men's violence and renegotiating the meaning of gender and sexuality and the balance of power between women and men at all levels of society.

1. Introduction

For decades women's organizations around the world have worked against gender-based violence through advocacy, victim services, and consciousness-raising. Largely because of their efforts, violence against women has recently been recognized as a legitimate human rights issue by the United Nations and by some governments. Yet almost no policy attention has been given to addressing violence against women as a public health issue, and even less to tackling its underlying causes. Efforts to gain recognition of violence as an issue warranting international concern have been hampered by lack of population-based data on abuse and its health consequences. But the data that exist are nonetheless sufficient to justify increased attention to this neglected—yet important—women's health issue.

As difficult and intractable as other health issues are, violence against women may be even more so. Deeply embedded attitudes about male-female relations, social taboos against discussing "private matters" in public, and the lack of a "technological fix" all work against a solution. Although violence against women is almost universal, its patterns and their causes can be fully understood and remedied only in specific social and cultural contexts. Each society has mechanisms that legitimize, obscure, deny—and therefore perpetuate—violence. Even where a particular act of violence might be deplored, powerful social institutions—the state, families, normative systems that regulate gender relations—collude in maintaining the status quo. Thus victims often have a difficult time escaping violent relationships.

A variety of mechanisms, from oral traditions to formal educational and legal systems, define standards of acceptable behavior for men and women. These standards are learned from an early age in the family and reinforced by peer pressure, community institutions, and the mass media. In many societies children learn that males are dominant and that violence is an acceptable means of asserting power and resolving conflict. Women, as mothers and mothers-in-law, unwittingly perpetuate violence by socializing girls and boys to accept male dominance and by acquiescing throughout life to male demands.

Mothers teach their daughters to accept the roles that society assigns them, and they punish "deviant" behavior to ensure their sexual and social acceptance.

But violence is not inevitable. Cross-cultural research shows that, although violence against women is an integral part of virtually all cultures, there are societies in which gender-based abuse does not exist (Sanday 1981; Levinson 1989). Such societies stand as proof that social relations can be organized in a way that minimizes or eliminates violence against women. Even where violence remains endemic, strategic intervention by the state, the community, and women's organizations can save lives, reduce injury, and lessen the long-term effects of victimization on women and their children. Existing interventions need to be refined and systematically evaluated, and new approaches to prevention explored, but it is wrong to conclude that nothing can be done to combat violence against women.

Women's organizations and, more recently, some governments have done much to assist victims and to document and publicize violence against women. Virtually everywhere these efforts have encountered strong resistance from organized religion, health professionals, the judicial system, and the police, all of whom see the home as sacrosanct and thereby tolerate—indeed condone—most of the violence against women and girls. Police in many countries will not intervene in "domestic quarrels" and do not consider wife beating a crime. In some courts men who confess to murdering their wives are acquitted in the name of "legitimate defense of honor." And women are frequently raped by the very men charged with their protection—the police, military officers, and other agents of the state.

Clearly, efforts to protect women must be strengthened and expanded at the local and national levels. But any strategy to combat violence must attack the root causes of the problem in addition to treating its symptoms. This means challenging the social attitudes and beliefs that undergird male violence and renegotiating the meaning of gender and sexuality and the balance of power between women and men at all levels of society.

Violence against women has evolved in part from a system of gender relations which posits that men are superior to women. The idea of male dominance—even male ownership of women—is present in most societies and reflected in their laws and customs. Thus violence should not be considered an aberration, but an extension of a continuum of beliefs that grants men the right to control women's behavior. As Fauveau and Blanchet observed in their pathbreaking study of violent deaths among women in Bangladesh:

> The underlying causes of violent deaths among women of reproductive age, i.e. complications of an induced abortion, suicide and homicide, are clearly social. Many of them may be seen as a consequence of the strict control enforced by males over the sexual life of women and reproduction. (1989, p. 1127)

Combating violence against women requires challenging the way that gender roles and power relations are articulated in society. To marshal support for such an effort, this paper draws together existing data on violence against women worldwide and reviews the literature on the health consequences of abuse. The paper describes the scope and evolution of the problem, reviews the health consequences of gender-based abuse, and provides a primer on violence against women. It then discusses the implications of gender violence for health and development and recommends steps toward eliminating the violence. Appendices recommend government actions to combat violence against women, discuss issues relating to defining such violence, and provide a methodology for estimating the global health burden from the abuse and rape of women. They also provide a sample "danger assessment" for screening women at risk and discuss treatment protocols for battered women.

Breaking the cycle of abuse will require concerted action across several sectors, including education, mass media, the legislative system, the judiciary, and the health sector. Appendix A provides detailed suggestions for action in each of these sectors.

2. The scope and evolution of the problem

In the past decade violence against women has become increasingly recognized as deserving international concern and action. Women's organizations around the world embraced gender violence as a priority issue during the United Nations Decade for Women (1975 to 1985). The United Nations (UN) General Assembly passed its first resolution on violence against women in November 1985. Since then, the UN has sponsored several Expert Group Meetings on Violence against Women and pursued the issue through its Commission on the Status of Women, the Economic and Social Council, the UN Statistical Office, and its Committee on Crime Prevention and Control. Recently two new international instruments have been put forward that would recognize all gender-based violence as an abuse of human rights—the UN Declaration on Violence against Women and the farther-reaching Draft Inter-American Convention to Prevent, Punish, and Eradicate Violence against Women (negotiated through the Organization of American States). Also, the Pan-American Health Organization has recognized gender-based violence as its priority theme for 1994 under its Women, Health, and Development Program, and the United Nations Fund for Women (UNIFEM) recently published a major document outlining the impact of gender violence on socioeconomic development (Carrillo 1992).

The growing international recognition of the importance of gender-based abuse comes on the heels of almost two decades of organizing by women's groups to draw attention to the issue. Women have been saying in a multiplicity of ways that violence is a major concern for them (box 1). Recently more than 200 women's nongovernmental organizations (NGOs) combined forces to protest violence against women during "Sixteen Days of Activism against Gender Violence" (November 25 to December 10). During this annual event groups sponsor workshops, conferences, and street theater and organize media coverage to raise public awareness of gender violence and to demand a response from public officials.

Definition of violence against women

In September 1992 the United Nations Commission on the Status of Women convened a special working group to draft a declaration against violence against women. This declaration, adopted by the General Assembly in the fall of 1993, offers for the first time an official UN definition of gender-based abuse. According to Article 1 of the declaration, violence against women includes:

> any act of gender-based violence that results in, or is likely to result in, physical, sexual or psychological harm or suffering to women, including threats of such acts, coercion or arbitrary deprivations of liberty, whether occurring in public or private life. (Economic and Social Council 1992)

Article 2 of the declaration states that the definition should be understood to encompass, but not be limited to, physical, sexual, and psychological violence occurring in the family and in the community, including battering, sexual abuse of female children, dowry-related violence, marital rape, female genital mutilation and other traditional practices harmful to women, nonspousal violence, violence related to exploitation, sexual harassment, and intimidation at work, in educational institutions, and elsewhere, trafficking in women, forced prostitution, and violence perpetrated or condoned by the state.

Significantly, this definition recognizes both physical and psychological harm and threats of such harm in both the public and the private sphere. The definition also refers specifically to the gender-based roots of such violence. In this paper we use the United Nations definition, but we also include a discussion of definitional issues in appendix B. The catalogue of abuses in the UN definition is not exhaustive, nor does it presume to be. For the sake of brevity, the paper will not address in depth certain forms of violence, including forced prostitution, sexual harassment, trafficking in women, or violence perpetrated by the state. This omission in no way reflects the relative importance of these issues. In fact, all forms of gender-based violence have common roots and can best be understood as points on a spectrum.

Dimensions of the problem

Accurately estimating the global health burden of violence against women is hampered by lack of data on the incidence and the health impact of abuse. Crime statistics are virtually useless in estimating the incidence of gender-based abuse because of gross underreporting. According to recent victimization surveys in the United States, only 2 percent of intrafamilial child sexual abuse, 6 percent of extrafamilial sexual abuse, and 5 to 8 percent of adult sexual assault cases are reported to the police. By comparison, 61.5 percent of robberies and 82.5 percent of burglaries are reported (Koss 1990). Nonetheless, significant progress has been made in recent years in estimating the prevalence of wife abuse in both industrial and developing countries. Because of the stigma associated with sexual violation, data on rape and sexual abuse are less easily collected, although large-scale epidemiologic surveys of sexual assault are beginning to emerge in industrial countries.

The following section reviews the data available on the different types of violence covered in this report: abuse of women, sexual assault, sexual abuse of children, neglect of girl children, and culture-bound practices that are harmful to women. Box 2 presents an overview of violence as it occurs through the life cycle. A life-cycle approach to gender-based victimization provides important insights into the immediate as well as the cumulative effects of violence on the lives of women and girls. Violence can occur during any phase of a woman's life; many women experience multiple episodes of violence throughout their lives. A life-cycle perspective also reveals that violence experienced in one phase can have long-term effects that predispose the victim to severe secondary health risks, such as suicide, depression, and substance abuse. Evidence suggests that the earlier in a woman's life violence occurs—especially sexual violence—the deeper and more enduring are its effects (Burnam and others 1988).

Prevalence of abuse by intimate partners

The most endemic form of violence against women is wife abuse—or, more accurately, abuse of women by intimate male partners. The 35 studies from a wide variety of countries summarized in table 1 show that in many countries one-quarter to more than half of women report having been physically abused by a present or former partner. An even larger percentage have been subjected to ongoing emotional and psychological abuse, a form of violence that many battered women consider worse than physical abuse. Although some of these studies are based on convenience samples, most are based on probability samples with a large number of respondents (Colombia, Kenya, Mexico, the United States).

Box 1 Evidence of women's interest in gender-based violence

When MATCH International, a Canadian funding organization, surveyed women's groups in developing countries for suggestions on future funding priorities, violence against women was the number one reply (Carrillo 1992).

At a recent 12-country workshop held in China on women's nonformal education, participants were asked to name the worst aspect of being female. The almost unanimous answer was fear of men's violence (Bradley 1990).

At a recent meeting on women's reproductive health in Asia, sponsored by the Population Council and the Indonesian Epidemiology Network, violence was identified as one of two priority areas (Population Council 1991).

At the November 1991 biannual conference of the Association of Women in Development, international participants identified violence against women as one of their five priority health concerns. More abstracts were submitted on issues relating to violence than on any other single theme (Marcelo 1992).

The National Black Women's Health Project has identified violence as the number one health issue for African American women in the United States (Avery 1990).

Women around the world collected more than 400,000 signatures (representing 124 countries) on a petition demanding that the United Nations Human Rights Conference held in June 1993 recognize violence against women as an abuse of women's human rights (Center for Women's Global Leadership 1993).

When the National Council for Women's Rights in Brazil sponsored a meeting in 1986 to develop a list of women's demands for the upcoming constitution-writing process, women demanded a new constitutional clause recognizing violence against women (Pitanguy, personal communication, 1993).

Each of the studies is individually valid, but they are not directly comparable because each uses a different set of questions to probe for abuse. Most of the studies ask the respondents whether they have been "abused," "beaten," or "involved in a violent relationship." A subset (the studies from Barbados, Chile, and the United States) makes this determination using a list of "acts" that a woman may or may not have been subjected to during her lifetime (being hit with an object or fist, being bitten).[1] Clinical and research experience suggests that question formats that require a woman to self-identify as abused generally underestimate the physical and psychological violence in intimate relationships.[2] In many cultures women are socialized to accept physical and emotional chastisement as a husband's marital prerogative, limiting the range of behavior they consider abuse. Moreover, women are sometimes reluctant to report abuse out of shame or out of fear of incriminating other family members. Both factors suggest that the prevalence rates in table 1 likely underestimate the abuse of women.

Prevalence of rape and sexual assault

Statistics from around the world suggest that sexual coercion is common in the lives of women and girls. Six well-designed studies from the United States, for example, suggest that between one in five and one in seven U.S. women will be the victim of a completed rape in her lifetime (Koss 1993; Kilpatrick, Edmunds, and Seymour 1992).[3] The U.S. data are consistent with studies of rape in other parts of the world. Studies of rape among college-age women in Canada, New Zealand, the United Kingdom, and the United States reveal remarkably similar rates of completed rape across countries (DeKeseredy and Kelly 1993; Gavey 1991; Beattie 1992; Koss, Gidycz, and Wisniewski 1987; table 2). A study among adult women (many of them college students) in Seoul, Korea, yielded a slightly lower rate of completed rape, but an equally high rate of attempted rape (Shim 1992). All of these studies used adaptations of the same survey instrument, based on the Sexual Experiences Survey (SES) by Koss and Oros (1982).

The estimates in table 2 are based on legal definitions of rape in the United States, which recognize as rape the penetration of any orifice by physical force or threat of force, or because a woman is incapacitated due to drugs or alcohol. (For comparison, the U.K. data include forced anal and oral penetration, although the legal definition of rape in the United Kingdom includes only vaginal penetration by a penis.)

Women have also been subjected, throughout history, to repeated and especially brutal rape as part of war. In recent years mass rape in war has been documented in

---

Box 2 Gender violence throughout the life cycle

Phase	Type of violence present
Prebirth	Sex-selective abortion (China, India, Republic of Korea); battering during pregnancy (emotional and physical effects on the woman; effects on birth outcome); coerced pregnancy (for example, mass rape in war).
Infancy	Female infanticide; emotional and physical abuse; differential access to food and medical care for girl infants.
Girlhood	Child marriage; genital mutilation; sexual abuse by family members and strangers; differential access to food and medical care; child prostitution.
Adolescence	Dating and courtship violence (for example, acid throwing in Bangladesh, date rape in the United States); economically coerced sex (African secondary school girls having to take up with "sugar daddies" to afford school fees); sexual abuse in the workplace; rape; sexual harassment; forced prostitution; trafficking in women.
Reproductive age	Abuse of women by intimate male partners; marital rape; dowry abuse and murders; partner homicide; psychological abuse; sexual abuse in the workplace; sexual harassment; rape; abuse of women with disabilities.
Elderly	Abuse of widows; elder abuse (in the United States, the only country where data are now available, elder abuse affects mostly of women).

Table 1 Prevalence of wife abuse, selected countries

Country	Sample	Sample type	Findings	Comment
Antigua (Handwerker 1993b)	97 women age 20 to 45	Random subset of national probability sample	30 percent of women battered as adults	50 percent of women and men report that their mothers were beaten
Barbados (Handwerker 1993a)	264 women and 243 men age 20 to 45	Islandwide national probability sample	30 percent of women battered as adults	50 percent of women and men report that their mothers were beaten
Belgium (Bruynnooghe and others 1989)	956 women between the ages of 30 and 40	Random sample from 62 municipalities throughout the country	3 percent had experienced very serious violence, 13 percent moderately serious violence, and 25 percent less serious violence	Survey queried women on 15 types of physical violence ranging from blows with the hand to life-threatening forms such as strangulation and gun wounds
Canada (Haskell and Randall 1993)	Face-to-face interviews with 402 women between the ages of 18 and 64 in Toronto	Random sample of all residential addresses (including apartments) in Toronto	27 percent report being ever physically assaulted by an intimate partner	36 percent of women reporting abuse report fearing that they would be killed by the man who assaulted them
Canada (Kennedy and Dutton 1989)	1,045 men and women in province of Alberta	454 face-to-face interviews with residents of households randomly selected from census enumerations; 244 telephone interviews with residents of Calgary and 347 with residents in rest of province, selected by random-digit dialing	11.2 percent of respondents report physical abuse within past year	This is a one-year rate
Canada (Lupri 1989)	426 married or cohabiting women	Random sample using face-to-face interviews and mailed questionnaires	17.8 percent of women report physical violence by a partner within the past year	This is a one-year rate
Canada (Smith 1987)	604 presently or formerly married or cohabitating women age 18 to 50 in metropolitan Toronto	Phone survey using random-digit dialing	36.4 percent report ever being physically abused in a relationship; 11.3 percent report severe physical abuse	14.4 percent report physical abuse within the past year
Canada (Statistics Canada 1993)	Nationally representative sample of 12,300 women 18 and older	In-depth interview by phone using random-digit dialing	25 percent of women (29 percent of ever-married women) report being physically assaulted by a current or former male partner since age 16	65 percent of victims were assaulted more than once, 32 percent more than 11 times; 45 percent of wife assault incidents resulted in injury

Country	Sample	Sample type	Findings	Comment
Chile (Larrain 1993)	1,000 women in Santiago age 22 to 55 involved in a relationship for 2 years or more	Stratified random sample with a maximum sampling error of 3 percent	60 percent have been abused by a male intimate; 26.2 percent have been physically abused (severe violence —that is, more severe than pushes, slaps, or having object thrown at them)	70 percent of those abused are abused more than once a year
Colombia (PROFAMILIA 1990)	3,272 urban women, 2,118 rural women	National random sample	20 percent physically abused; 33 percent psychologically abused; 10 percent raped by husband	Part of Colombia's Demographic and Health Survey
Costa Rica (Chacon and others 1990)	1,388 women	Convenience sample of women attending child welfare clinic	54 percent report being physically abused	Sponsored by UNICEF/PAHO
Ecuador (CEPLAES 1992)	200 low-income women	Convenience sample of Quito barrio	60 percent had been beaten by a partner	37 percent of those beaten were assaulted from once a month to every day
Guatemala (1990 study by Frederico Coy, cited in Castillo and others 1992)	1,000 women	Random sample of women in Sacatepequez	49 percent abused, 74 percent by an intimate male partner	Includes physical, emotional, and sexual abuse in adulthood; sponsored by UNICEF/PAHO
India (Mahajan 1990)	109 men and 109 women from village in Jullundur District, Punjab	50 percent sample of all scheduled-caste households and 50 percent of non-scheduled-caste households	75 percent of scheduled-caste men admit to beating their wives; 22 percent of higher-caste men admit to beatings	75 percent of scheduled- (lower-) caste wives report being beaten frequently
India (Rao 1993)	170 women of childbearing age in 3 villages in rural southern Karnataka	100 percent sample of potter community in each village based on previous census	22 percent of women report being physically assaulted by their husbands; 12 percent report being beaten within the past month, on average 2.65 times	Author notes that informal interviews and ethnographic data suggest that prevalence rates are "vastly under-reported"
Japan (Domestic Violence Research Group 1993)	796 women from all over Japan (17 percent return on 4,675 questionnaires)	Convenience sample based on survey distributed nationally through women's groups, adult education classes, media, etc.	58.7 percent report physical abuse by a partner; 65.7 percent report emotional abuse; 59.4 percent report sexual abuse	44 percent of sample experienced all three types of abuse simultaneously. This is not a representative sample
Kenya (Raikes 1990)	733 women from Kissi District	Districtwide cluster sample	42 percent beaten regularly	Taken from contraceptive prevalence survey

Country	Sample	Sample type	Findings	Comment
Korea, Rep. of (Kim and Cho 1992)	707 women and 609 men who had lived with a partner for at least two years	Three-stage, stratified random sample of entire country; face-to-face interviews	37.5 percent of wives report being battered by their spouse in last year	12.4 percent report serious physical abuse within last year
Korea, Rep. of (Shim 1988)	708 women in Suwon and Seoul	Convenience sample; based on distributed questionnaires	42.2 percent have been beaten by husband after marriage	14 percent report being beaten by their husband within the last year
Malaysia (WAO 1992)	713 women and 508 men over 15	National random sample of Peninsular Malaysia	39 percent of women were physically beaten by a partner in 1989	15 percent of adults (22 percent of Malays) consider wife beating acceptable
Mexico (Ramirez and Vazquez forthcoming)	1,163 rural women and 427 urban women in the state of Jalisco	Random household survey of women on DIF (social welfare) register	56.7 percent of urban women and 44.2 percent of rural women had experienced some form of interpersonal violence	In more than 60 percent of cases the principal aggressor was the husband
Mexico (Shrader Cox and Valdez Santiago 1992)	342 women age 15 or older, low- to middle-income	Random sample of households in Mexico City peri-urban neighborhood	33 percent had lived in a violent relationship; 6 percent had experienced marital rape	Of abused women, 66 percent had been physically abused, 76 percent psychologically abused, and 21 percent sexually abused
Netherlands (Romkens 1989)	1,016 women age 20 to 60	Face-to-face interviews	20.8 percent had experienced physical violence in a heterosexual relationship	Half of those reporting abuse (11 percent) had experienced severe, repeated violence
New Zealand (Anderson and others forthcoming)	3,000 women in Otago sent questionnaire; 497 women interviewed (half sexually abused and half control group)	Random sample of women selected from electoral rolls; all figures weighted back from interview sample to main postal sample	22.4 percent had been physically abused since age 16, 76 percent by a male intimate (17 percent of total)	20.7 percent of those physically abused by a partner were also sexually abused in the relationship
New Zealand (Mullen and others 1988)	2,000 women sent questionnaire; stratified random sample of 349 women selected for interview	Random sample selected from electoral rolls of five contiguous parliamentary constituencies	20.1 percent report being hit and physically abused by a male partner; 58 percent of these women (>10 percent of sample) were battered more than 3 times	

Country	Sample	Sample type	Findings	Comment
Norway (Schei and Bakketeig 1989)	150 women age 20 to 49 in Trondheim	Random sample selected from census data	25 percent had been physically or sexually abused by a male partner	Definition includes only forms of violence more severe than pushing, slapping, or shoving
Papua New Guinea (Toft 1986)	*Rural:* 736 men, 715 women	Rural survey in 19 villages in all regions and provinces	67 percent of rural women beaten	Almost perfect agreement between percentage of women who claim to have been beaten and percentage of men who admit to abuse
	Urban: low-income, 368 men, 298 women; *elites,* 178 men, 99 women	Urban survey with oversample of elites	56 percent of urban low-income women beaten; 62 percent of urban elite women beaten	
Sri Lanka (Sonali 1990)	200 low-income women from various ethnic groups in Colombo	Convenience sample from low-income neighborhood	60 percent have been beaten	51 percent said husbands used weapons
Tanzania (Sheikh-Hashim and Gabba 1990)	300 women from Dar es Salaam	Convenience sample from three districts —Ilala, Temeke, and Kinondoni (interviews)	60 percent had been physically abused by a partner	
Uganda (Wakabi and Mwesigye 1991)	80 women (16 from each of Kampala's five divisions)	House-to-house written survey; 7 women refused to answer	46 percent of 73 women responding reported being physically abused by a partner	An additional 7 women reported beatings by family members and another 5 assaults or rapes by outsiders
United States (Grant, Preda, and Martin 1989)	6,000 women statewide in Texas sent questionnaires; 1,539 usable questionnaires returned	Statewide random sample based on women holding valid driver's licenses	39 percent have been abused by male partner since age 18; 31 percent have been physically abused	More than 12 percent have been sexually abused by male partner since age 18
United States (Straus and Gelles 1986)	2,143 married or cohabiting couples	National probability sample using random-digit dialing	28 percent report at least one episode of physical violence	11.3 percent report abuse within past year
United States (Teske and Parker 1983)	3,000 rural women in Texas sent questionnaires	Random sample from communities of 50,000 or less	40.2 percent have been abused since age 18; 31 percent have been physically abused	22 percent abused within the past 12 months
Zambia (Phiri 1992)	171 women age 20 to 40	Convenience sample of women from shanty compounds, medium- and high-density suburbs of Lusaka and Kafue Rural	40 percent beaten by a partner; another 40 percent mentally abused	17 percent said they thought that physical or mental abuse was a normal part of marriage

Table 2 Prevalence of rape among college-age women, selected countries

Country	Study authors	Sample	Definition of rape used [a]	Rate of completed rape	Rate of completed and attempted rape
Canada	DeKeseredy and Kelly 1993	National probability sample of 1,835 women at 95 colleges and universities	Anal, oral, or vaginal intercourse by force or threat of force SES 9,10	8.1 percent (by dating partners since high school)	23.3 percent (rape or sexual assault by anyone ever)
New Zealand	Gavey 1991	347 female psychology students (convenience sample)	Anal, oral, or vaginal intercourse by force or threat, or because a man gave alcohol or drugs SES 8,9,10	14.1 percent	25.3 percent
United Kingdom	Beattie 1992	1,476 women at 22 universities and polytechnics (convenience sample)	Anal, oral, or vaginal intercourse by force or because a man gave alcohol or drugs SES 8,9,10	11.7 percent	19.4 percent
United States	Koss, Gidycz, and Wisniewski 1987	Representative sample of 3,187 women at 32 colleges and universities	SES 8,9,10	15.4 percent (since age 14)	27.5 percent
United States	Moore, Nord, and Peterson 1989	Nationally representative sample of 18- to 22-year-olds	Forced to have sex against will, or raped	12.7 percent of whites; 8 percent of blacks (before age 21)	
Seoul, Republic of Korea	Shim 1992	2,270 adult women (quota sample)	SES 9,10	7.7 percent	21.8 percent

a. SES numbers indicate which of the following questions taken from the Sexual Experiences Survey (Koss and Oros 1982) were used in the study to estimate rates of rape and attempted rape:

4. Has a man attempted sexual intercourse (getting on top of you, attempting to insert his penis) when you didn't want to by threatening or using some degree of physical force (twisting your arm, holding you down, etc.), but intercourse did not occur?
8. Have you had sexual intercourse when you didn't want to because a man gave you alcohol or drugs?
9. Have you had sexual intercourse when you didn't want to because a man threatened or used some degree of physical force (twisting your arm, holding you down, etc.) to make you?
10. Have you engaged in sex acts (anal or oral intercourse or penetration by objects other than a penis) when you didn't want to because a man threatened or used some degree of physical force (twisting your arm, holding you down, etc.) to make you?

Bosnia, Cambodia, Liberia, Peru, Somalia, and Uganda (Swiss and Giller 1993). A European Community fact-finding team estimates that more than 20,000 Muslim women have been raped in Bosnia since the fighting began in April 1992. Many have been held in "rape camps" where they have been raped repeatedly and forced to bear Serbian children against their will (Post 1993). These examples notwithstanding, rape in war is neither a new phenomenon nor one limited to developing countries.

Prevalence of child and adolescent sexual abuse

Because the sexual abuse of children is such a sensitive issue, there are few population-based studies from which its prevalence can be estimated. The few studies that do exist and ample indirect evidence suggest that sexual abuse of children and adolescents is widespread. In the United States, for example, studies show that 27 to 62 percent of women recall at least one incident of sexual abuse that occurred before they were 18 (Peters, Wyatt, and Finkelhor 1986).[4] An anonymous, island-wide probability survey in Barbados revealed that one woman in three and one to two men in 100 report having been subject to behavior constituting childhood or adolescent sexual abuse (Handwerker 1993a).[5] In Canada a government commission estimated that one in four female children and one in 10 male children are sexually assaulted before age 17 (Badgely 1984).

The indirect evidence available elsewhere also suggests cause for concern. Two studies from Nigeria documenting sexually transmitted diseases (STDs) in very young children suggest that sexual abuse is at least present in Nigerian society. A 1988 study in Zaria, Nigeria, found that 16 percent of female patients seeking treatment for STDs were children under age five and another 6 percent children between ages six and 15 (Kisekka and Otesanya 1988). An older study in Ibadan found that 22 percent of female patients attending one STD clinic were children under age 10 (Sogbetun, Alausa, and Osoba 1977). In Peru a study conducted in the Maternity Hospital of Lima revealed that 90 percent of the young mothers age 12 to 16 had been raped—the vast majority by their father, their stepfather, or another close relative (Rosas 1992). An organization for adolescent mothers in Costa Rica reports similar findings: 95 percent of its pregnant clients under 15 are victims of incest (Treguear and Carro 1991).

This indirect evidence is consistent with cross-cultural data from rape crisis centers which reveal that 40 to 58 percent of sexual assaults are perpetrated against girls age 15 and under, including girls younger than 10 or 11.[6] Most of these rapes are committed by family members or other persons whom the victim knows. In fact, justice statistics and data from rape crisis centers show that in more than 60 percent of all rape cases the victim knows the perpetrator (table 3). The common perception of rape as a "stranger" crime is sorrily misguided.

A final indication of the prevalence of sexual abuse comes from the observations of children themselves. In 1991, when Centro de Información y Servicios de Asesoría en la Salud (CISAS), a Nicaraguan health NGO, held a national conference for the children involved in their CHILD to Child program (a project that trains youngsters age 8 to 15 to be better child care providers for their siblings), participants identified physical and sexual abuse as the most important health problem that young people in their country faced. Since then, CISAS has helped initiate a national campaign to educate the public about sexual abuse of children ("Rompiendo el Silencio," 1992).

Prevalence of discriminatory treatment and infanticide

The preference for sons common in many cultures can have serious consequences for the health and lives of females. Studies show that where this preference is strong and resources are scarce, girls receive less food, education, and medical care than boys. In rural Bangladesh malnutrition was found to be almost three times more common among girls than among boys (Bhatia 1985; Chen, Huq, and D'Souza 1981). Even more striking are differences in access to health care. In Matlab, Bangladesh, boys outnumber girls at diarrheal treatment centers by 66 percent, even though both sexes get diarrhea with equal frequency (Bhatia 1985).

Not surprisingly, this discriminatory treatment shows up in mortality statistics for girls and women. In 45 developing countries for which recent data are available, the mortality rate among girls age one to four is higher than that among boys in this age group in all but two countries (UNICEF 1986). Discrimination against girl children is so strong in the state of Punjab in India, for example, that girls age two to four die at twice the rate that boys in this age group do (Das Gupta 1987). According to a World Bank report, "deaths of young girls in India exceed those of young boys by almost one third of a million every year. Every sixth infant death is specifically due to gender discrimination" (Chatterjee 1990).

In some parts of the world the preference for male children is so strong that parents eliminate girl children through infanticide or selective abortion. A 1987 census

Table 3 Statistics on sexual crimes, selected countries

	Percentage of perpetrators known to victim	Percentage of victims age 15 and under	Percentage of victims age 10 and under
Lima, Peru	60	—	18[a]
Malaysia	68	58	18[b]
Mexico City	67	36	23
Panama City	63	40	—
Papua New Guinea	—	47	13[c]
Santiago, Chile[d]	72	58	32[e]
United States	78	62[e]	29

— Not available.
Note: Except for the U.S. data, which cover only completed rapes, data include rape and sexual assaults, such as attempted rape and molestation.
a. Percentage of survivors age nine and younger.
b. Percentage of survivors age six and younger.
c. Percentage of survivors age seven and younger.
d. Based on five-year averages derived from crimes reported to the Legal Medicine Service, 1987-91, as published in *Anuario Estadístico del Servicio Medico Legal de Chile* (as cited in Avendaño and Vergara 1992).
e. Percentage of survivors age 17 and younger.
Source: Data for Malaysia from Consumer's Association 1988; data for Panama City from Perez 1990; data for Peru from Portugal 1988; data for Papua New Guinea from Riley, Wohlfahrt, and Carrad 1985, as cited in Bradley 1990; data for Mexico City from COVAC 1990 and Procurador de Justicia del Distrito Federal de Mexico 1990; data for Chile cited in Avendaño and Vergara 1992; data for United States from Kilpatrick, Edmunds, and Seymour 1992.

survey by the State Statistical Bureau of China showed that there were half a million fewer female infants than one would predict given the expected biological ratio of male to female births. A detailed analysis of the census data, published in the *Population and Development Review,* shows that the ratio of males to females has been rising since 1982 (Hull 1990). The missing female infants represent mainly second- and third-order births in rural areas. Both these observations strongly suggest that the one child policy implemented in 1979 in China has led to either increased female infanticide or the selective abortion of female fetuses.[7]

Other studies confirm that in China, India, and the Republic of Korea access to amniocentesis and ultrasound is sufficiently widespread that feticide could in fact be skewing the male-female sex ratios (Coale and Banister 1992).[8] Genetic testing for sex selection has become a flourishing business in India, especially in the north. Until protests from women's organizations stopped blatant promotion of the testing, Indian sex detection clinics advertised that it was better to spend $38 now on terminating a female fetus than $3,800 later on her dowry. One study of amniocentesis in a large Bombay hospital found that 95.5 percent of fetuses identified as female were aborted, compared with only a small percentage of male fetuses (Ramanamma 1990).

Studies in remote regions of southern India also confirm the persistence of female infanticide. In a prospective study of all births within a 12-village region of Tamil Nadu, nutritionist Sabu George of Cornell University found that 58 percent of deaths (19 of 33) among female infants were due to infanticide. The girls were most often killed within seven days of birth; the two most common methods were to feed them the poisonous sap of a plant and to choke them by lodging rice hulls soaked in milk in their throats. There were no male infanticides during the two-and-half-year study (George, Abel, and Miller 1992).

An analysis first advanced by Harvard economist Amartya Sen and later refined by demographer Ansley Coale offers a simple but powerful illustration of the cumulative impact of these factors on women's survival prospects. Sen and Coale compared the sex ratios in countries where both sexes receive similar care, such as countries in Europe and North America, with those in countries where females are severely discriminated against, such as China and India. The female-male ratio in the first group of countries is about 1.05 or 1.06, reflecting women's biological advantage. But in South Asia, West Asia, North Africa, and China the ratio is typically 0.94 or lower. If these regions had the sex ratio typical of countries in which there is less gender discrimination (including some Sub-Saharan African countries), there would be more than 60 million more

females alive today. The "missing women" are victims of feticide, infanticide, selective malnourishment, lack of investment in women's health, and various forms of gender violence (Sen 1990; Coale 1991).[9]

Prevalence of culture-bound practices harmful to women

A variety of other practices can reasonably fall under the rubric of gender violence if that term is defined to link physical and mental harm to women with male power and control. In this section we advance the term "culture-bound practices harmful to women" as a replacement for the phrase commonly used in the United Nations system, "traditional practices harmful to women."

In UN parlance *traditional practices* refers primarily to such practices as genital mutilation and child marriage. Although these practices are known to have negative consequences for women's health and well-being, they are undertaken, often with women's collusion, to make girls more acceptable marriage partners.

We suggest broadening this concept to include harmful practices and behaviors common in industrial societies which are likewise motivated by a desire to make women into acceptable, attractive sexual partners for men. These include pathological dieting (anorexia and bulimia) and high-risk cosmetic surgery. There are, of course, significant differences among these practices, not the least of which is that genital mutilation is generally performed on children, with or without their consent. Nonetheless, we feel that genital mutilation should be viewed as one point on a continuum of harmful practices motivated by women's desire to conform to socially prescribed standards of beauty and marriageability.

Best estimates indicate that 85 million to 114 million girls and women in the world have undergone genital mutilation. Most of these girls and women live in Africa, a few live in Asia, and an increasing number live in Europe, Canada, and the United States, as immigrant and refugee families import the practice (Toubia 1993). Genital mutilation—frequently called female circumcision—is a broad term applied to a range of practices involving the removal of all or part of the clitoris and other external genitalia. In its most severe form, known as infibulation, the clitoris and both labia are removed and the two sides of the vulva are sewn together, leaving only a small opening to allow urine and menstrual blood to pass. In its less extreme form, all or part of the clitoris is removed (clitoridectomy) or the clitoris and inner lips are removed (excision). About 85 percent of women who are mutilated undergo one of the two less severe operations.

Many observers trace the origins of genital mutilation to a desire to control female sexuality and to preserve the virginity of young girls until marriage (Hedley and Dorkenoo 1992). A host of superstitions help perpetuate the practice, but the core belief driving the tradition is that men will not marry uncircumcised women, believing them to be promiscuous, unclean, and sexually untrustworthy (Mohamud 1991).

In other societies in which virginity at marriage is considered absolutely essential, girls are often married off at extremely young ages, frequently to men many years their senior. Recent Demographic and Health Surveys from the developing world indicate that, although child marriage is declining, a large percentage of young girls are still married off before their fifteenth birthday (table 4). Not uncommonly, these child brides are traumatized by adult sex and forced to bear children before their bodies are fully mature. A common side effect of too-early childbearing is vesico-vaginal or recto-vaginal fistula—a tearing of the walls between the vagina and the bladder or rectum—due to prolonged obstructed labor and lack of access to health care (birth control, prenatal care, or surgical intervention). Women with unrepaired fistulae constantly drip urine and feces, making them social outcasts and likely candidates for divorce or abandonment.

Elsewhere young girls and women themselves put their health at risk—by severely restricting their dietary intake. In North America and Europe surveys of adolescent women suggest that roughly one of every 100 to 200 young women suffer from anorexia. This psychological disorder, restricted almost exclusively to girls and women in western industrial societies and Japan, is characterized by extreme weight loss induced through gradual self-starvation (Gordon 1990). As dieting transforms into fasting and finally into willful starvation, the anorexic typically withdraws from ordinary activities and relationships and intensifies an already excessive exercise routine. She becomes obsessed with dieting and counting calories and with the sight of her own image in the mirror.

Bulimia—a different but related disorder—is characterized by binge eating accompanied by purging through self-induced vomiting or ingestion of laxatives. Estimates using the most stringent criteria (binging and purging on a weekly basis, and a preoccupation with shape and body weight) put the prevalence of bulimia among U.S. high school and college females at between 3 and 5 percent, suggesting that several million young American women have a clinically significant problem with bulimia. The incidence of bulimia, like that of anorexia nervosa, has been increasing throughout the western world, a trend corresponding to the growing emphasis on thinness as a cultural and sexual ideal (Gordon 1990; Brumberg 1988).[10]

The same cultural obsessions with thinness and socially defined notions of beauty that promote eating disorders are prompting women in some western societies to seek cosmetic surgery, often at considerable risk to their physical health. An estimated 2 million U.S. women have undergone breast enlargement surgery, at an average cost of about $4,000 per operation. Amid much controversy, the U.S. Food and Drug Administration recently prohibited the use of silicone breast implants for cosmetic purposes, fearing that the products of silicone breakdown could be carcinogenic (implants may still be used for breast reconstruction after mastectomies). There is also concern that silicone implants complicate detection of breast cancer and may be linked to certain autoimmune diseases.

Table 4 Women age 20 to 24 today who were married before age 15, selected countries

Country	Percent	Year of report
Mali	21.3	1989/90
Nigeria	26.7	1990
Cameroon	26.7	1987
Uganda	17.8	1991
Liberia	16.6	1986
Egypt[a]	15.0	1987
Pakistan	11.4	1991
Indonesia	10.0	1987
Guatemala	12.6	1987
Dominican Republic	9.0	1988
Mexico	6.2	1991
Trinidad and Tobago	6.0	1990/91

a. Before age 16.
Source: Selected Demographic and Health Surveys.

3. A primer on violence against women

Many beliefs about violence against women are untrue. These same beliefs, despite their inaccuracy, have been used to avoid recognition of the problem and prevent investments in solutions. To dispel such misperceptions, women's groups have prepared lists of truths about domestic violence representing the collective wisdom of those working on issues of gender-based violence. This section outlines some of the most common of these truths and presents data supporting them. For the sake of brevity, it offers only a few examples in support of each.

Women are most at risk of violence from men they know

Contrary to the view of the family as a haven of love and support, data from around the world suggest that girls and women are at greater risk of violence in their homes than anywhere else. A 1987 study of more than 2,000 battery cases registered during five months at the Sao Paulo Women's Police Station, for example, found that more than 70 percent of all reported incidents of violence against women took place in the home. In almost all the cases the abuser was the woman's husband or lover. More than 40 percent involved serious bodily injury (Americas Watch 1991).

This finding was confirmed by Brazil's 1988 national household survey (PNAD), conducted by the Brazilian Institute for Geography and Statistics (IBGE). The survey found that Brazilian men who were murdered or physically abused were attacked outside the home primarily by an acquaintance or stranger; Brazilian women, by contrast, were murdered by their intimates. Among cases of abuse of men, only 10 percent involved relatives (including spouses); women were related to their abuser in more than half the reported cases of physical violence (Americas Watch 1991). Fifty percent of the rapes reported to Brazil's 125 women's police stations between January 1991 and August 1992 were committed by family members (Dimenstein 1992).

A recent review of violence against women in the United States, published in the *Journal of the American Medical Association*, observes that "studies now document that women in the United States are more likely to be assaulted and injured, raped, or killed by a current or ex-male partner than by all other types of assailants combined" (Council on Scientific Affairs 1992, p. 3185). A study in Colombia in the early 1980s by the Forensic Institute of Bogotá found that a fifth of the cases of bodily injury presented to the forensic physician for assessment were due to conjugal violence, and 94 percent of those hospitalized were battered women (United Nations 1991). And a study evaluating medical records from a public hospital emergency room and two clinics in Santiago, Chile, found that of the 2,618 women seen for assault-related injuries from September through November 1986, 1,884 (73 percent) were injured by family members (United Nations 1989).

Gender violence cuts across all socioeconomic groups

Although studies suggest that violence against women is more prevalent among poor and working-class families, they also consistently show that violence occurs in all socioeconomic and educational classes, although not at the same prevalence rates.

Violence within the family is at least as injurious as assaults by strangers

Violence between intimates is often considered less dangerous than street violence; in reality the opposite is often true. In the United States more than 80 percent of all assaults committed by spouses and former spouses result in injuries, compared with 54 percent of assaults by strangers. Victims of marital violence have the highest rates of internal injuries and unconsciousness (Lentzner and DeBerry 1980, as cited in the Council on Scientific Affairs 1992).

Though women can be violent, most violence that causes injury is perpetrated by men against women

According to the Uniform Crime Reports, in the United States men constitute 83 percent of all offenders arrested, 99 percent of those charged with rape, and 86 percent of those charged with offenses against family and children (Flanagan and McGarrell 1986, as cited in Koss 1990). Victimization surveys show that more than 90 percent of adult rape victims in the United States are women (National Victimization Survey, as cited in Koss 1990). And in an analysis of the results of the U.S. National Crime Surveys of 1973-82 Schwartz concludes that "there are...more than 13 times as many women [as men] seeking medical care from a private physician for injuries received in a spousal assault" (Schwartz 1987, p. 67, as cited in Dobash and others 1992).

The 1981 Canadian Urban Victimization Survey and the 1987 General Social Survey also found that women were the primary victims of assaults by intimates (Solicitor General of Canada 1985; Sacco and Johnson 1990; Statistics Canada 1990). In a review of the data from these surveys Johnson (1989) concluded that "women account for 80-90 percent of victims in assaults or sexual assault between spouses or former spouses. In fact, the number of domestic assaults involving males was too low in both surveys to provide reliable estimates."

The "gendered" nature of most violent crime is especially evident in murder statistics. In most nations, between 80 and 90 percent of homicide offenders are male. An even higher share of those whose victims are adult women are male: in Canada about 95 percent of the killers of women (females 15 and older) are male (Gartner and McCarthy 1991).

Contrary to this pattern, women constitute a significant share of those who neglect or physically abuse their children—in part because women generally bear primary responsibility for the care and discipline of young children. The victims of physical abuse are as likely to be boys as they are girls. This is not the case, however, with child sexual abuse: the vast majority of abuse is directed at young girls by older men. In the United States 78 percent of substantiated cases of child sexual abuse involve girls (Wyatt and Powell 1988). In Durban, South Africa, of 37 Indian victims of child sexual abuse identified at R. K. Khan Hospital, 92 percent were girls. All but one of the perpetrators were male, and two-thirds were male family members (Haffejee 1991). And in Costa Rica service statistics show that 94 percent of victims of child sexual abuse are girls and 96 percent of the perpetrators are male (Claramunt 1991).

Violence within relationships tends to escalate over time

Women's groups providing services to victims of domestic violence in both the industrial and the developing world confirm that abuse within relationships tends to be multifaceted and to escalate over time. The best available data illustrating the point are from the United States. Consider the following:

- Studies of abused women in the United States have shown that the majority—73 to 85 percent—do not experience physical violence until they have married. After they marry, the frequency and severity of violence tends to escalate (Browne 1987).
- Data from two representative surveys in Texas demonstrate a pattern of multiple abuse. Of the women who reported being physically abused after age 18, 74.6 percent also suffered specific types of emotional abuse and 34.3 percent suffered sexual abuse (Teske and Parker 1983; Grant, Preda, and Martin 1989).
- In a study at Yale University Hospital, Stark and Flitcraft found that nearly one in five battered women had presented at least 11 times with trauma; another 23 percent had brought six to 10 abuse-related injuries to the attention of clinicians. In most of these cases the health care provider never identified the history of abuse underlying the injuries (Stark and others 1981).

Most violent men are not mentally ill, contrary to common perception

Studies of abusive men in the United States indicate that few exhibit diagnosable psychopathology (Maiuro and others 1988); among those who do, there is no consistent pattern of illness (Bograd 1984). Indeed, the pervasiveness of violence against women suggests that men who abuse women and girls are not mentally ill. Many abusive men are merely exerting what they see as their natural right to dominate women.

Emotional and psychological abuse can be at least as debilitating as physical abuse

Those who work with victims of domestic violence report that women often consider psychological abuse and humiliation more devastating than physical assault. A detailed study of 127 battered women in Ireland that asked the question "What was the worst aspect of the battering experience?" received the following top five responses: mental torture (30), living in fear and terror (27), the physical violence (27), depression or loss of all confidence (18), and effects on children (17; Casey 1988).

*Alcohol exacerbates but does not cause
violence against women*

In a few societies and subcultures wife abuse seems to occur mainly in conjunction with abuse of alcohol or drugs, or both, but in many others alcohol is seldom involved. In a study of 90 small-scale societies Levinson (1989) found eight in which men's use of alcohol is a key component in the sequence of events leading up to wife-beating incidents and five in which both alcohol-related and non-alcohol-related abuse is reported. In the 77 other societies alcohol use plays little or no part in abuse.

Research in the United States shows that abusive men with severe alcohol problems abuse their partners both when they are drunk and when they are sober; these men are also violent more frequently, and inflict more serious injuries on their partners, than abusive men without alcohol problems (Frieze and Browne 1989). Thus treating an underlying alcohol problem can help reduce the incidence and severity of assaults, but it seldom ends the violence. Often both men and women use the supposed disinhibiting effects of alcohol to excuse behavior that otherwise would not be tolerated.

*There are societies in which violence
against women does not exist*

Although violence against women is an integral part of virtually all cultures, there are reports of societies in which gender-based abuse does not exist. In his ethnographic review of 90 peasant and small-scale societies, Levinson (1989) identifies 16 that can be described as "essentially free [of] or untroubled by family violence." And Sanday (1981) has found that there are societies free of rape. Such cultures—even if few in number—offer proof that violence against women is not inevitable.

4. Health consequences of gender-based violence

A growing body of research has emerged in recent years on the mental and physical health consequences of violence against women and the burden it places on health care systems. Although much of this research is from the industrial world, clinicians and advocates in developing countries confirm that the U.S.-based literature corresponds well to their experience with battered women and survivors of sexual assault and abuse.

When this literature is considered together with estimates of the prevalence of gender-based violence in different parts of the world, the magnitude of the violence-related health burden begins to become clear. Perhaps the best estimate of this burden comes from a modeling exercise undertaken by the World Bank to inform its policy annual, the *World Development Report*, which in 1993 focused on health. For this effort, Bank staff and outside experts estimated the healthy years of life lost to men and women due to different causes. The exercise counted every year lost due to premature death as one disability-adjusted life year (DALY) and every year spent sick or incapacitated as a fraction of a DALY, with the value depending on the severity of the disability.

From this analysis, broken down by region and age group, rape and domestic violence emerge as a significant cause of disability and death among women of reproductive age in both the industrial and the developing world (see appendix C). In established market economies gender-based victimization accounts for nearly one in five healthy years of life lost to women age 15 to 44. On a per capita basis the health burden of rape and domestic violence affecting reproductive-age women is roughly the same in industrial and developing countries, but because the overall burden of disease is much greater in developing countries, a smaller percentage is attributable to gender-based victimization.

The World Bank estimates that rape and domestic violence account for 5 percent of the healthy years of life lost to women of reproductive age in demographically developing countries. In developing countries such as China, where maternal mortality and poverty-related diseases are relatively under control, the healthy years

of life lost due to rape and domestic violence again account for a larger share—16 percent of the total burden. At a global level the health burden from gender-based victimization among women age 15 to 44 is comparable to that posed by other risk factors and diseases already high on the world agenda, including the human immunodeficiency virus (HIV), tuberculosis, sepsis during childbirth, cancer, and cardiovascular disease (table 5).

The following section explores the long- and short-term health effects of different types of abuse. Box 3 presents the range of health effects recorded in the literature.

Table 5 Estimated global health burden of selected conditions for women age 15 to 44

Condition	Disability-adjusted life years lost (millions)
Maternal conditions	29.0
Sepsis	10.0
Obstructed labor	7.8
STDs (excluding HIV)	15.8
Pelvic inflammatory disease	12.8
Tuberculosis	10.9
HIV	10.6
Cardiovascular disease	10.5
Rape and domestic violence[a]	9.5
All cancers	9.0
Breast	1.4
Cervical	1.0
Motor vehicle accidents	4.2
War	2.7
Malaria	2.3

a. Rape and domestic violence are included here for illustrative purposes. They are *risk factors* for disease conditions, such as STDs, depression, and injuries, not diseases in and of themselves.
Source: World Bank 1993.

Health effects of abuse by intimate partners

Abuse of women by intimate male partners has both physical and mental health consequences. The physical consequences include injury and a host of less-defined somatic complaints. In the United States 22 to 35 percent of women presenting to urban emergency rooms exhibit symptoms related to ongoing abuse (Council on Scientific Affairs, American Medical Association 1992). A representative survey of women in Texas found that 24 percent of women who had ever been abused required medical treatment because of the abuse (Teske and Parker 1983).

Abuse-related injuries include bruises, cuts, black eyes, concussions, and broken bones. Abuse also leads to miscarriages and to permanent injuries, such as damage to joints, partial loss of hearing or vision, and scars from burns, bites, and knife wounds. In Bangladesh and parts of Latin America acid throwing, a form of abuse increasingly perpetrated by vengeful lovers, leads to permanent disfigurement. In addition to injuries, battered women often suffer chronic headaches, abdominal pains, muscle aches, recurrent vaginal infections, and sleep and eating disorders. Two studies, one covering 390 randomly selected women in the United States and the other 2,000 randomly selected women in New Zealand, found that abused women had significantly worse physical and mental health than nonabused women (Koss, Koss, and Woodruff 1991; Mullen and others 1988). Recent research reported in the *Journal of the American Medical Association* suggests that abuse can also be associated with delayed physical effects, particularly arthritis, hypertension, and heart disease (Council on Scientific Affairs 1992).

Quantitative data on health consequences in developing countries are less available, but abundant evidence from crisis centers, police reports, and ethnographic research shows that in these countries, too, violence is a significant cause of injury and ill health. The case study presented by China to the United Nations Expert Group Meeting on Violence in the Family reports that domestic violence caused 6 percent of deaths and serious injuries in Shanghai in 1984 (Wu 1986). A three-month surveillance survey in Alexandria, Egypt, indicated that domestic violence was the leading cause of injury to women, accounting for 27.9 percent of all visits by women to area trauma units (Graitcer, personal communication, 1994). And 18 percent of married women surveyed in urban areas of Papua New Guinea (PNG) had received hospital treatment for injuries inflicted by their husbands. As Christine Bradley of the country's law reform committee observes: "In PNG, where many women have enlarged spleens due to malaria, a single blow can kill them" (1988, p. 3).

For many women, however, the psychological effects of abuse are more debilitating than the physical effects. Fear, anxiety, fatigue, post-traumatic stress disorder

---

Box 3 Health consequences of gender-based violence

NONFATAL OUTCOMES

Physical health consequences

STDs
Injury
Pelvic inflammatory disease
Unwanted pregnancy
Miscarriage
Chronic pelvic pain
Headaches
Gynecological problems
Alcohol/drug abuse
Asthma
Irritable bowel syndrome
Injurious health behaviors
   (smoking, unprotected sex)
Partial or permanent disability

Mental health consequences

Post-traumatic stress disorder
Depression
Anxiety
Sexual dysfunction
Eating disorders
Multiple personality
   disorder
Obsessive-compulsive
   disorder

FATAL OUTCOMES

Suicide
Homicide

(PTSD),[11] and sleeping and eating disturbances are common long-term reactions to violence. Abused women may become dependent and suggestible, and they may find it difficult to make decisions alone. Compounding the psychological consequences that women suffer from abuse is their relationship to the abuser. The legal, financial, and emotional ties that the victims of marital violence often have to the perpetrator enhance their feelings of vulnerability, loss, betrayal, and hopelessness. Abused women frequently become isolated and withdrawn as they try to hide the evidence of their abuse.

Not surprisingly, these effects make wife abuse a primary context for many other health problems. Battered women in the United States are four to five times more likely than nonbattered women to require psychiatric treatment and five times more likely to attempt suicide (Stark and Flitcraft 1991). About a third of battered women suffer major depressions, and some go on to abuse alcohol or drugs.[12] Miller (1990) reports that spousal violence is the strongest predictor of alcoholism in women, even after controlling for income, violence in the family of origin, and having an alcoholic husband. Moreover, studies show that most battered women who drink begin drinking excessively only after the onset of abuse (Amaro and others 1990; Stark and others 1981).

The relation between battering and psychological dysfunction also has important implications for women's mortality, because of increased risk of suicide. After reviewing evidence from the United States, Stark and Flitcraft concluded that "abuse may be the single most important precipitant for female suicide attempts yet identified" (1991, p. 141). One-fourth of suicide attempts by American women—and half of all attempts by African-American women—are preceded by abuse (Stark 1984).

A cross-cultural survey of suicide by Counts draws the same conclusion, positing that in some African, Oceanic, and South American societies, female suicide operates as a culturally recognized behavior that enables the "politically powerless...to revenge themselves on those who have made their lives intolerable" (1987, p. 195). Counts finds support for her argument in cultures from Africa, Peru, Papua New Guinea, and the Melanesian islands. Among Fijian Indian families in which someone has committed suicide, 41 percent cite marital violence as the cause (Haynes 1984).

Suicide is not an inconsequential form of death. The World Bank estimates that of the healthy years of life lost to women in rural China, 30 percent are lost due to suicide (Bobadilla, personal communication, 1993). This finding is consistent with reports of mass suicides in rural China among women forced or sold into unwanted (and often violent) marriages (name withheld 1991). In Sri Lanka, a country with reasonably accurate mortality statistics, the rate of death due to suicide among young women age 15 to 24 is five times that due to infectious diseases and 55 times the rate due to obstetric-related causes (WHO 1985).

Three studies from India suggest a similar link between marital violence and female suicide. A one-year study of completed suicides in Delhi revealed that 46 percent were committed by males and 54 percent by females. It cited marital discord and ill treatment by husbands and in-laws as the most common precipitating factor among women. Another study analyzed all cases of suicide in 1978 known to the Madras Police Department. The peak ages for women committing suicide were 15 to 20. Among the two-thirds of the women who were married, the principal cause cited for suicide was "maladjustment with an alcoholic or drug-addict husband." The third study, on

suicide deaths in Daspur, found that the peak ages for women were 15 to 24 and the most common precipitating factor was "quarrel with spouse" (as cited in Paltiel 1987).

The relation between domestic violence and homicide may be even more profound. Data from a wide range of countries demonstrate that domestic violence is a major risk factor for murder of and by women. A recent review of spousal homicide in the United States, published in the *American Journal of Public Health,* reports that "studies of homicides between intimates show that they are often preceded by a history of physical abuse directed at the women and several studies have documented that a high proportion of women imprisoned for killing a husband had been physically abused by their spouses" (Mercy and Saltzman 1989, p. 597). In Canada 62 percent of women murdered in 1987 died at the hands of an intimate male partner (Canadian Centre for Justice Statistics 1988). In the first 11 months of 1992, 415 women were murdered in the Brazilian state of Pernambuco, 70 percent by a male intimate (Dimenstein 1992). Of the 100 murders in Israel (not including the territories) in 1991, 42 involved women killed by a husband or lover (Nevo 1993). And in Papua New Guinea almost 73 percent of adult women murdered between 1979 and 1982 were killed by their husbands (Bradley 1988). Studies from a variety of cultures—including Canada, Papua New Guinea, and the United States—confirm that when women kill men, it is often in self-defense and usually after years of persistent and escalating abuse (Browne 1987; Walker 1989; Canadian Centre for Justice Statistics 1988; Bradley 1988; Kellerman and Mercy 1992).

The link between intimate violence and homicide is particularly evident in India, where women's deaths due to burns have been increasing since 1979, a development that can be tied to the commercialization of dowry demands (Pawar 1990). A young bride may be subject to severe abuse from her husband and in-laws if their continuing demands for money or goods from her family are not met. A frequent subterfuge is to set the woman on fire with kerosene and then claim that she died in a kitchen accident— hence the term bride-burning. In 1990 the police officially recorded 4,835 dowry deaths in India, but government sources readily acknowledge that this is a gross underestimate (Kelkar 1992). In both urban Maharashtra and greater Bombay, one of every five deaths among women age 15 to 44 is due to "accidental burns." For the younger age group 15 to 24, the proportion is one of four (Karkal 1985).

Health effects of rape and sexual assault

Sexual assaults can cause both physical injury and profound emotional trauma. A study of rape in urban and rural areas of Bangladesh reports that 84 percent of victims suffered severe injuries or unconsciousness, mental illness, or death following the rape (Shamim 1985). Rape survivors exhibit a variety of trauma-induced symptoms—nightmares, depression, inability to concentrate, sleep and eating disturbances, and feelings of anger, humiliation, and self-blame. In addition, 50 to 60 percent of victims experience severe sexual problems, including fear of sex, problems with arousal, and decreased sexual functioning (Burnam and others 1988; Becker and others 1986; Becker and others 1982).

The malignant effects of rape are not surprising given the physical, psychological, and moral violation of the person that it represents (Breslau and others 1991; Herman 1992). A study from the United States found that rape victims were nine times more likely than nonvictims to have attempted suicide, and twice as likely to experience a major depression (Kilpatrick 1990). Follow-up studies have shown that rape survivors have higher rates of persistent post-traumatic stress disorder (PTSD) than victims of other traumas (Norris 1992). Some experts consider female victims of sexual abuse and assault to be the largest single group of PTSD sufferers, and rape the single most likely event to cause PTSD (Foa, Olasov, and Steketee 1987).

Studies that follow victims over time show that the traumatic consequences of rape can persist for many years. A study to validate the Rape Aftermath Symptom Test (RAST) demonstrated that the instrument could distinguish the symptoms of rape victims from those of nonvictims at intervals up to three years after a rape (Kilpatrick 1988). According to studies in the United States, one in four women who have been raped still exhibits dysfunctional symptoms four to six years after the assault (Hanson 1990; Burgess and Holmstrom 1979). In another sample 60 percent of sexual assault victims reported sexual dysfunction three years after the assault (Becker and others 1986). Even after many years, women who have been sexually assaulted are significantly more likely to qualify for 10 different psychiatric diagnoses, including major depression, alcohol abuse, PTSD, drug abuse, obsessive-compulsive disorder, generalized anxiety, eating disorders, multiple personality disorder, and borderline personality syndrome. The relative risk ratio for these diagnoses for survivors of rape and sexual assault is about two times greater risk (Koss 1990).

Beyond physical injury and emotional trauma, rape survivors face the risk of sexually transmitted diseases (STDs), including the acquired immunodeficiency syndrome (AIDS). A support center for rape victims in Bangkok, Thailand, reports that 10 percent of its clients contract a sexually transmitted disease as a result of the rape (Archavanitkui and Pramualratana 1990). In the United States almost a dozen women and twice as many children had contracted AIDS through rape and child sexual abuse by July 1992 (Dattel 1992).

The possibility of unwanted pregnancy is also

substantial. Mexican rape crisis centers report that 15 to 18 percent of their clients become pregnant because of rape, a figure consistent with data from Korea and Thailand (COVAC 1990; CAMVAC 1985; Archavanitkui and Pramualratana 1990; Shim 1992). Rape victims in Mexico have more options than victims in many other countries: a new law requires judges to rule on a rape survivor's request for an abortion within five working days. But in countries in which abortion is illegal even in cases of rape, or where safe abortion services are inaccessible or prohibitively expensive, thousands of women must suffer the double humiliation of being raped and then being compelled to bear the rapist's child.

The consequences of rape for victims in societies that place a high value on women's virginity are severe. Many African, Asian, and Middle Eastern cultures equate a young woman's worth with her virginity. As Fauveau and Blanchet describe in their ground-breaking study of injury in rural Bangladesh, "even when women are victims, a premarital sexual relation is said to spoil something intrinsic in their physical and moral person....Their ruined reputation cannot be mended" (1989, p. 1125). The study cites numerous case studies of women who were beaten, murdered, or driven to suicide because of the dishonor that rape or illegitimate pregnancy brought upon their families. Their study found that there were 130 percent more deaths from injury (suicide, homicide, assault, and complications from induced abortion) among unmarried than among married teenage girls; this reinforces their qualitative data suggesting deliberate violence toward girls who are raped or who become pregnant outside of marriage (Acasadi and Johnson-Acasadi 1990). Likewise, in a study of female homicides in Alexandria, Egypt, 47.1 percent of women who had been killed had been murdered by a relative after they had been raped (Graitcer and Youssef 1993).

Health effects of child and adolescent sexual abuse

Research in the United States has shown that about one-fifth of child sexual abuse victims evidence serious long-term psychological effects (Browne and Finkelhor 1986). These may include disassociative responses and other PTSD indicators, such as chronic arousal, nightmares, flashbacks, and emotional numbing. Burnam and others (1988), using multivariate techniques, demonstrated that women in the Los Angeles Epidemiological Catchment Area survey who were sexually abused as children were more than twice as likely as peers who were not abused (58.6 percent versus 24.0 percent) to have at least one psychiatric diagnosis in their lifetime. (The L.A. Catchment survey is an ongoing mental health research project sponsored by the National Institutes of Mental Health.) Victims who were abused by fathers or stepfathers, whose assaults involved genital contact, and whose molestation involved force appear to be at especially high risk of long-lasting effects (Browne and Finkelhor 1986).

Fully distinguishing the physical and emotional effects of sexual abuse is difficult because the long-term psychological complications are often manifested as physical complaints. Limited research into the somatic consequences of child sexual abuse indicates that it is linked to chronic pelvic pain, headaches, asthma, and gynecological problems (Koss and Heslet 1992). Recent research has also linked sexual abuse with such gastrointestinal disorders as irritable bowel syndrome and chronic abdominal pain. These disorders, which have no clearly established pathogenesis, occur more frequently in women than in men, and they pose a considerable health and economic burden. In the United States they are the most common chronic gastrointestinal diagnoses seen in primary care and gastroenterology practices (Drossman and others 1990).

Early sexual victimization may also leave women less skilled at protecting themselves, less sure of their worth and their personal boundaries, and more apt to accept victimization as a part of being female. These effects may increase the chances of future victimization (Koss 1990). Early traumatic sexual experiences have been linked to increased risk for rape among college women (Koss and Dinero 1989). Likewise, in Briere's community-based sample, 49 percent of childhood sexual abuse victims reported being battered in adult relationships, compared with 18 percent of the nonvictim group (Briere 1984, as cited in Browne and Finkelhor 1986). Russell (1986) found that 68 percent of incest victims reported being the victim of rape or attempted rape (excluding incestuous rape) later in their lives, compared with 17 percent of nonabused controls.

Recent studies also link early sexual victimization with high-risk behaviors in adolescence and adulthood, including excessive drug and alcohol use, unprotected sex with multiple partners, prostitution, and teen pregnancy (Zierler and others 1991; Finkelhor 1987; James and Meyerding 1977; Boyer and Fine 1992). A variety of studies link childhood abuse to the later development of alcoholism, especially in women (Dembo 1987; Jellinek, Murphy, and Poitrast 1992; Blane, Miller, and Leonard 1988). A particularly well-designed multiple-regression analysis by Miller, Downs, and Testa (forthcoming) found that rates of childhood victimization were significantly greater for women in alcoholism treatment programs than for women in treatment for other mental health problems, battered women without alcohol problems, or nonalcoholic women in the general population. These findings remained significant even after controlling for demographic and family background differences, including parental alcohol problems.

Researchers Debra Boyer and David Fine (1992)

likewise found a significant link between childhood sexual abuse and teenage pregnancy among a sample of 535 adolescent mothers in Washington State. Compared with teens who became pregnant but had not been abused, sexually abused adolescents began intercourse a year earlier, were more likely to have used drugs and alcohol, and were less likely to practice contraception. Abused adolescents were also more likely to have been battered by an intimate partner and to have exchanged sex for money, drugs, or a place to stay. The average age at first intercourse for abused women was 13.8 years, compared with the national average of 16.2. Only 28 percent of the abused teens used birth control at first intercourse, compared with 49 percent of their peers.

Health effects of genital mutilation

The medical complications of genital mutilation can be severe, especially for women who are infibulated. A study from Sierra Leone found that 83 percent of all women circumcised required medical attention at some time for problems related to the procedure (Hosken 1988). The immediate risks of clitoridectomy or infibulation are similar: hemorrhage of the clitoral artery, infection, urine retention, and tetanus or blood poisoning from unsterile and often primitive cutting implements (knife, razor blade, broken glass). And the pain of the operation, often carried out without anesthesia, can cause young girls to go into shock.

Over the long term women who are infibulated generally suffer more severe physical health consequences than women who are excised. Infibulation, because it involves more extensive cutting and stitching, poses significantly higher risks of hemorrhage and infection. And the partial closing of the vaginal and urethral openings leads to more problems relating to retention of urine and menstrual blood, such as chronic urinary tract infections, stones in the urethra or bladder, constant back and menstrual pain, irregularity, and repeated reproductive tract infections. In some cases these infections can lead to sterility, a devastating consequence for women whose worth is defined largely in terms of their ability to bear children.

Infibulation destines a woman to a cycle of pain, cutting, and restitching to accommodate sexual intimacy and childbirth. Infibulated women often must be cut on their wedding night to make intercourse possible, and again for the birth of a child. Intercourse is frequently perceived as painful, a perception that likely has both physical and psychological roots. And at the time of birth, infibulation puts both mother and child at risk. Among 33 infibulated mothers followed at Somalia's Benadir Hospital, all required extensive episiotomies during childbirth, their second-stage labor was five times longer than normal, five of their babies died, and 21 suffered oxygen deprivation because of the long and obstructed labor (Warsame 1988). Most women are reinfibulated after childbirth to reconstruct a small vaginal opening; over time this repeated cutting and stitching transforms the genital area into tough, unyielding scar tissue.

Although excised women normally have fewer long-term complications than women who are infibulated, clitoridectomy is not without serious risks. A significant share of excised women face a lifetime of unending infections, pain, bleeding, and abscesses. They also face the possibility of severe psychological repercussions. Little research has been done on the psychological impact of genital mutilation, but clinicians report serious long-term distress and psychological dysfunction in some cases. Based on her experience in Sudan, Dr. Nahid Toubia describes a pattern of vague physical complaints, depression, and lethargy among circumcised women very similar to that common among sexually abused or raped women in the United States:

> Thousands of women [in Sudan] come to the Ob/Gyn outpatient clinics with vague chronic symptoms which they metaphorically interpret as originating from the pelvis. These women are perceived by doctors and the hospital authorities as a great nuisance and a drain on the system since they have no medically detectable pathology. Sitting for hours listening to them, it soon becomes clear that the vague symptoms of general fatigue, loss of sleep, backache, headache, pelvic congestion, uttered in a depressed, monotonal voice, are a muted cry for help for a much more deeply felt pain. With a little probing, the women talk about fear of sex, the threat of infertility after infection, and fears about the state of their genitals (they have no way of assessing whether they are normal). (Toubia 1993, p. 19)

In 1982 the World Health Organization (WHO) issued a statement warning that genital mutilation should never be carried out by professional health staff. Despite this statement and many similar resolutions drafted by various medical bodies, delegates to the UN Human Rights Seminar on Traditional Practices held in Burkina Faso in 1991 reported that, for reasons of financial gain, medical personnel are performing circumcisions in hospitals in place of the midwives and traditional practitioners who normally carry out the procedure (Dorkenoo and Scilla 1992). Although "medicalizing" circumcision may reduce the immediate risks of infection, it does not end the abuse of women's human rights represented by this unnecessary, mutilating surgery. As Aziza Kamil, leader of the Cairo Family Planning Association's project on female genital mutilation, points out:

> No action will entrench genital mutilation more than legitimating it through the medical profession. If doctors and hospitals start to perform it, rather than condemn it, we will have no hope of ever eradicating the practice. All the respect and authority given to doctors will be transferred to the practice and [activists] will lose [their] credibility. (Dorkenoo and Scilla 1992)

Effects of violence against women on the health care system

Violence affects women's health—and the health of society at large—by diverting scarce resources to the treatment of a largely preventable social ill. Considering the prevalence of abuse and the nature of its health effects, it is reasonable to conclude that victimization represents a significant drain on available health resources. A study at a major U.S. health maintenance organization (HMO) found that a history of rape or assault was a stronger predictor of physician visits and outpatient costs than any other variable, including a woman's age or such health risks as smoking (Koss, Koss, and Woodruff 1991). This multiple-regression analysis, which included five demographic variables, four measures of health status, and five measures of lifetime stress, found the following:

- Women who had been raped or beaten had medical costs in the index year that were two and a half times higher than those of women who were not victimized ($401 versus $161).
- According to a temporal analysis based on a subset of victims, the biggest increase in use of health care services occurred in the second year following victimization, but four years after the incident it still had not returned to baseline.
- Women who have been assaulted or raped describe themselves as less healthy, experience more symptoms across virtually all body systems (except skin and eyes), and report higher rates of behaviors injurious to the health (such as smoking and failure to use seat belts).

A similar study by Felitti (1991) found that among women enrolled in an HMO plan, 22 percent of those who had a history of childhood molestation or rape had visited a physician 10 or more times a year, compared with only 6 percent of nonvictimized women. And in a random, population-based survey of medical care use in Los Angeles, respondents with a history of sexual assault were nearly twice as likely to have sought mental health care and a third more likely to have visited a physician within the past six months than men and women who had not been sexually assaulted (Golding and others 1988). This effect persisted even after gender, ethnicity, and age were controlled for. The study's multivariate analysis suggests that assault has an indirect influence, affecting health care use by increasing psychiatric morbidity and reducing functional ability. The study also demonstrates that the prevalence of sexual assault is significantly higher among those who use health services than among those who do not, underlining the importance of using health care facilities to identify victims of violence for referral for appropriate advocacy and support.

5. Implications of gender violence for health and development

Gender violence has important implications for socio-economic development and for key initiatives already high on the international health agenda. Yet few mainstream development organizations, even among those devoted to health issues, have focused on violence. The World Health Organization and a handful of NGOS have supported efforts to eliminate genital mutilation, but such abuses as battery, rape, and incest have been largely ignored. The Women, Health and Development program of the Pan-American Health Organization (PAHO) and the Canadian NGO MATCH International are notable exceptions.

Effect on socioeconomic development

Gender violence, through its effects on a woman's ability to act in the world, can serve as a brake on socioeconomic development. The development community has come to realize that such problems as high fertility, deforestation, and hunger cannot be solved without women's full participation. Yet women cannot lend their labor or creative ideas fully when they are burdened with the physical and psychological scars of abuse.

New evidence from the United States suggests that the scars of victimization can also lead to lower future educational attainment and income levels for women who are abused. Using simultaneous equations to model the income effects of childhood sexual abuse, Batya Hyman (1993) has shown that women who have been abused earn 3 to 20 percent less each year than women who have not been abused, with the discrepancy depending on the type of sexual abuse experienced and the number of perpetrators (the model controls for all other factors known to affect income prospects). Incestuous abuse affected income indirectly through its impact on educational attainment and mental and physical health status. Women sexually abused by strangers suffered an additional direct effect on income; Hyman speculates that they learn from this abuse that the outside world is dangerous, and therefore limit their engagement in the world.

Violence against women can also thwart the development of the wider community through its effect on women's participation in development projects. A study commissioned by UNIFEM/Mexico to find out why women stopped participating in projects found that threats from men were a major cause. Men perceived the growing empowerment of their wives as a threat to their control, and used beatings to try to reverse this process of empowerment. In Madras, India, a revolving loan fund of the Working Women's Forum almost collapsed after the project leaders, subjected to increased domestic violence, stopped participating (Carrillo 1992). As Dr. Christine Bradley, Principal Project Officer for the Papua New Guinea Law Reform Commission, observes:

> Simply attending a meeting may be dangerous for a woman whose husband does not want her to go. In [Papua New Guinea] some husbands prevent their wives from attending meetings by locking them in the house, or by pulling them off the vehicle they have boarded to take them to the meeting, or even by pursuing them to the meeting and dragging them home. (Bradley 1990, p. 5)

In a particularly gruesome example of male backlash, a female leader of the highly successful government-sponsored Women's Development Programme in Rajasthan, India, was recently gang raped by male community members because they disapproved of her organizing efforts against child marriage. They raped the woman in her home in front of her husband, and warned him "Keep your wife in line or we'll rape her again." The incident and the fear that it induced dealt a major blow to the project's momentum (Rao Gupta, personal communication, 1993; Mathur 1992).

Elsewhere, men may use force to divert the benefits of development from women. Case studies of victims of domestic violence in Peru and of garment workers in the Mexican *maquiladoras* reported that men frequently beat their wives to get their earnings (Vasquez and Tamayo 1989, as quoted in Carrillo 1992).

To avoid violence, women learn to restrict their behavior to what they think will be acceptable to their husbands or partners. As Bradley (1990) observes, "Threats or fears of violence control women's minds as much as do acts of violence, making women their own jailers." In Papua New Guinea, for example, a recent study reports that married female teachers do not apply for or accept promotions in large part because they fear retaliation from their husbands: women represent only 39 percent of the country's primary school teachers and 5 percent of head teachers (Gibson 1990).

Fear of stranger-perpetrated violence similarly limits women's participation in public life. In the United States 49 percent of 299 women surveyed in six neighborhoods in Chicago, Philadelphia, and San Francisco estimated their chances of being raped in their own neighborhood as five or higher on a 10-point scale. Nearly half said that they relied on restrictive, isolating tactics (not going out, not going to certain places) "all or most of the time" or "fairly often" to protect themselves. By contrast, 90 percent of men living in the same neighborhoods said that they never restricted their behavior out of fear (Gordon and Riger 1989). Similarly, in a 1990 newspaper survey in Seoul, Korea, women identified fear of sexual violence as a principal cause of stress in their lives (Korea Sexual Violence Relief Center 1991). In a separate survey of 2,270 Korean women, 94 percent said that they felt uneasy because of the spread of sexual violence against women. Forty percent felt "extremely uneasy" and reported restricting their activities because of their fear (Korea Sexual Violence Relief Center 1991).

In the developing world this distinctly female fear can have unexpected and insidious effects. Fear of rape has exacerbated undernutrition among Ethiopian refugee families in Sudanese border camps. In a recent survey of women's mental health sponsored by the United Nations Development Programme, Ethiopian refugee women said that they had reduced the number of cooked meals they fed their children because they feared being raped—as many had been—while collecting firewood, a task requiring a two-to-three-hour foray outside the camp (LaPin 1992). Similarly, female health promoters working in rural Gujurat, India, when discussing obstacles to their work, emphasized their reluctance to travel alone between villages for fear of being raped. They requested self-defense training to enable them to continue their work (Khanna 1992). These examples, far from isolated, illustrate the paralyzing and largely unrecognized effect that violence can have on women and on social development.

Effect on maternal health

Pregnancy should be a time when the health and well-being of women are especially respected. But surveys suggest that pregnant women are prime targets for abuse. Results from a large prospective study of battery during pregnancy among low-income women in Baltimore and Houston indicated that one of every six pregnant women was battered during her present pregnancy (McFarlane and others 1992). The study, published in the *Journal of the American Medical Association,* followed a stratified cohort of 691 white, African-American, and Hispanic women for three years. Sixty percent of the abused women reported two or more episodes of violence, and they were three times as likely as nonabused women to begin prenatal care in the third trimester. Other studies indicate that, compared with women who are not beaten, women battered during pregnancy run twice the risk of miscarriage and four times the risk of having a low-birth-weight baby (Stark and others 1981; Bullock and McFarlane 1989). Low birth weight is a powerful predictor of a child's survival prospects in the first year of life.

In the developing world a survey of 342 randomly sampled women near Mexico City revealed that 20 percent of those battered reported blows to the stomach during pregnancy (Shrader Cox and Valdez Santiago 1992). And in a study of 80 battered women who sought judicial intervention against their partners in San Jose, Costa Rica, 49 percent reported being beaten during pregnancy. Of these, 7.5 percent reported miscarriages due to the abuse (Ugalde 1988). For mothers in developing countries who are already malnourished and overworked and lack access to adequate health care, battering during pregnancy is likely to have an even greater effect than for most women in industrial countries.

Violence may also be responsible for a sizable but unrecognized share of maternal mortality, especially among young unwed pregnant women. Fauveau and Blanchet (1989) report that in Matlab Thana, Bangladesh, homicide, and suicide motivated by the stigma of rape, pregnancy outside of marriage, or beatings or by dowry problems, accounted for 6 percent of 1,139 maternal deaths between 1976 and 1986.[13] The figure rises to 21.5 percent if deaths due to botched abortions are included, many of which are likewise related to shame over pregnancies outside of marriage. Among all deaths of women age 15 to 44 (not just maternal deaths), intentional injury accounts for 12.3 percent, with deaths due to homicide and suicide outnumbering those due to abortions.

Intentional injury was also found to be a significant cause of maternal deaths among women in Chicago, Illinois. Researchers examining the records of the Cook County Medical Examiner found that trauma was the number one cause of maternal deaths between January 1986 and December

1989, accounting for 46 percent of all maternal deaths. Of these, 57 percent were due to homicide and 9 percent to suicide (Fildes, Reed, and Jones 1992).

A prospective study of 161 women living in Santiago, Chile, revealed that women living in socially and politically violent areas had a significantly higher risk of pregnancy complications than women in less violent neighborhoods. After adjusting for potentially confounding variables (income, education, marital status, underweight, cigarette smoking, dissatisfaction with neighborhood, life events, alienation, uncertainty, and depression), researchers found that high levels of sociopolitical violence were associated with an approximately fivefold increase in risk of such pregnancy complications as pre-eclampsia, premature labor, threat of miscarriage, and gestational hypertension (Zapata and others 1992). If the stress and trauma of living in a violent neighborhood can induce complications, it is reasonable to assume that living in the private hell of an abusive relationship can produce similar sequelae.

Effect on family planning

Many women limit their use of contraception out of fear of male reprisal (Dixon-Mueller 1992). Men in many cultures reject birth control because they think it signals a woman's intention to be unfaithful, based on the logic that protection against pregnancy allows a woman to be promiscuous. And where fathering children is a sign of virility, a woman's request to use birth control may be interpreted as an affront to her partner's masculinity. Although the male partner's approval is not always the deciding factor, studies from countries as diverse as Bangladesh, Mexico, and South Africa have found that it was the single greatest predictor of women's contraceptive use.[14] When partners disapprove, women forgo contraception or resort to family planning methods they can use without their partner's knowledge.

The unspoken reality behind this subterfuge is that women can be abused if they do not comply with men's sexual and childbearing demands. In a recent interview Hope Mwesigye of FIDA-Uganda, a nonprofit legal aid organization for women in Kampala, recounted the story of a young married mother running from a husband who beat her regularly. Although he earned a decent wage, the woman's husband refused to maintain her and their two children. To avoid bringing into the world more children whom she could not feed, the woman began using birth control, without her husband's consent. When she failed to bring forth more children, the beatings began; they became more brutal when he learned that she was using contraceptives (Banwell 1990).

Where legal provisions require spousal permission before birth control can be dispensed, women can be at increased risk of violence. According to Pamela Onyango of Family Planning International Assistance, women in Kenya have been known to forge their partner's signature rather than risk violence or abandonment by requesting his permission to use family planning services (Banwell 1990). Researchers conducting focus groups on sexuality in Mexico and Peru found that women there similarly feared violence, desertion, or accusations of infidelity if they brought up birth control (Folch-Lyon, Macorra, and Schearer 1981; Fort 1989). Not surprisingly, when family planning clinics in Ethiopia stopped requiring spousal consent, use of the clinics rose 26 percent in just a few months (Cook and Maine 1987).

Not all women who fear violence because of using or discussing contraceptives are necessarily at risk of actual abuse. In fact, some studies suggest that many men may be more accepting of family planning than most women suspect (Gallen 1986). But communication in marriage is often so limited that women have no idea of their partner's view of family planning but assume that it mirrors the cultural norm—frequently that men want large families and distrust women who use birth control. The discrepancy between women's perceptions and reality also speaks to the way that violence induces fear by example.

Even in countries where birth control is generally accepted, violence can restrict a woman's ability to exercise reproductive and sexual autonomy. In a representative survey of women in Texas, more than 12 percent of the 1,539 respondents reported having been sexually abused by a husband, ex-husband, boyfriend, or ex-boyfriend after the age of 18. Of those 187 women, 12.3 percent stated that they had been prevented from using birth control and 10.7 percent that they had been forced to get pregnant against their will (Grant, Preda, and Martin 1989).

Studies from the United States suggest that sexual victimization may play an indirect role in perpetuating unwanted pregnancy. In a community-based, random survey of women in Los Angeles, Wyatt, Guthrie, and Notgrass (1992) found that women who were sexually abused in childhood were 2.4 times more likely to be sexually revictimized during adulthood; revictimized women, in turn, had a significantly higher rate of unintended and aborted pregnancies than non-revictimized women.

Boyer and Fine's (1992) study of adolescent mothers in Washington State, discussed above in the section on the health effects of child and adolescent sexual abuse, suggests that there are links between childhood sexual abuse and unwanted pregnancy among teenage women. Noting that concerted effort to improve teenagers' access to contraception and sex education had failed to reduce the rate of adolescent pregnancy in the United States over the past 20 years, the authors suggest that a "key factor in the conundrum of adolescent high-risk sexual behavior and adolescent pregnancy" (1992, p. 11) may be unresolved issues around early sexual victimization.

Effect on STD and AIDS prevention

Not surprisingly, male violence can impede women's ability to protect themselves from HIV and other sexually transmitted diseases (STDs). Violence can increase a woman's risk through nonconsensual sex or by limiting her willingness or ability to get her partner to use a condom. In many cultures suggesting condom use is even more threatening than raising birth control in general, because condoms are widely associated with promiscuity, prostitution, and disease. A woman's act of bringing up condom use can be perceived as insinuating her infidelity or implicitly challenging a male partner's right to conduct outside relationships. Either way, it may trigger a violent response (Worth 1989).

An AIDS prevention strategy based solely on "negotiating" condom use assumes an equity of power between men and women that simply does not exist in many relationships. Even in consensual unions, women often lack control over their sexual lives. A study of home-based industrial workers in Mexico, for example, found that wives' bargaining power in marriage was lowest with regard to decisions about whether and when to have sexual intercourse (Beneria and Roldan 1987). Studies of natural family planning in the Philippines, Peru, and Sri Lanka and of sexual attitudes among women in Guatemala report forced sex in marriage, especially when men arrive home drunk (Liskin 1981; Lundgren and others 1992). The summary of the Guatemalan study's focus groups observes that "it is clear from the replies the women gave...that being forced through violence to have sex by their partner is not an uncommon experience for Guatemalan women" (Lundgren and others 1992, p. 34).

For women who live with violent or alcoholic partners the possibility of coercive sex is even more pronounced. In the United States 10 to 14 percent of married women report being physically forced to have sex against their will, but among battered women the prevalence of coercive intercourse is at least 40 percent (Campbell and Alford 1989). In Bolivia and Puerto Rico 58 percent of battered wives report being sexually assaulted by their partner (ISIS International 1988), and in Colombia the reported rate is 46 percent (PROFAMILIA 1992). Given the percentage of women around the world who live with physically abusive partners, sexual coercion within consensual unions is probably common.

Childhood sexual abuse also puts individuals at increased risk of STDs, including AIDS, through the responses it generates in victims. Several studies link a history of sexual abuse with a high risk of entering prostitution (Finkelhor 1987; James and Meyerding 1977). Researchers from Brown University found that men and women who had been raped or forced to have sex during their childhood or adolescence were four times more likely than nonabused people to have worked in prostitution (Zierler and others 1991). They were also twice as likely to have multiple partners in any single year and to engage in casual sex with partners they did not know. Women survivors of childhood sexual assault were twice as likely to be heavy consumers of alcohol and nearly three times more likely to become pregnant before age 18. These behaviors did not translate directly into higher rates of HIV among women, but men who had experienced childhood sexual abuse were twice as likely to be HIV-positive as men who had not. The higher prevalence of HIV among male survivors could not be explained by a history of intravenous drug use.

Based on a probability survey of 407 men and women on Barbados, anthropologist Penn Handwerker has likewise shown that sexual abuse is the single most important determinant of high-risk sexual activity among Barbadian adolescents (Handwerker 1993a). After a wide range of socioeconomic and home-environment variables (for example, an absent father) are controlled for, sexual abuse remains strongly linked both to the number of partners adolescents have and to their age at first intercourse. Further analysis shows that the direct effects of childhood sexual abuse on a person's sexual behavior remain significant into the mid-thirties. For men, physical, emotional, and sexual abuse in childhood is also highly correlated with failure to use condoms in adulthood, after controlling for many other variables.[15]

There is some evidence that sexual abuse may affect women's risk of AIDS through its effect on their drug use (Fullilove, Lown, and Fullilove 1992; Paone and Chavkin 1993). In a qualitative study of women attending an outpatient methadone maintenance clinic in the South Bronx, early sexual abuse—especially incest—emerged as one of the most formative experiences in the lives of women addicted to drugs (crack, cocaine, heroin). As author Dooley Worth explains:

> The sense of stigmatization and shame experienced by female incest victims...leaves the young women feeling unloved, unlovable and *unable to say "no" to things they do not want to do such as having sex or using drugs.* (Worth 1991; emphasis in original)

Another effect of incest in girls is a tendency to disassociate from their bodies. This makes denial of risk-taking easier and leaves girls more vulnerable to peer pressure. With this constellation of effects, it is not surprising that researchers are finding links between childhood sexual abuse and such behaviors as intravenous drug use, alcohol abuse, and precocious sexuality (Worth 1991).

Effect on children

Children who witness wife abuse are at risk of being assaulted themselves and of developing adjustment problems during childhood and adolescence. In a study of battered women presenting to the Institute of Legal Medicine in Bogotá, Colombia, 74 percent of those who had children said that their children were present during the attack. In 49 percent of cases the children were also injured (Berenguer 1988). Of 80 women presenting to the Medico Forense of San Jose, Costa Rica, 40 percent said that their children were also beaten by their partner (Ugalde 1988). And in a representative survey of women in Texas, 33 percent of those abused during their lifetime had children who were abused by the same person (Teske and Parker 1983).

Perhaps even more significant than the physical injury that results from family violence is the effect it has on children's sense of security and their developing personalities. Two recent studies show that children who witness violence experience many of the same emotional and behavioral problems that abused children do, including depression, aggression, disobedience, nightmares, poor school performance, and somatic health complaints (Davis and Carlson 1987; Jaffe and others 1986).[16] And evidence from Canada and the United States suggests that children who witness or experience violence are more likely to be abusive as adults (Stordeur and Stille 1989).

But violence may affect child survival in another, more subtle way. It is well established that female education is significantly and independently related to child survival (Blumberg 1989). What is not yet clear is *how* education affects child health. There is increasing evidence that schooling works not by imparting new knowledge or skills relating to health, but by eroding fatalism, improving women's self-confidence, and changing the balance of power in the family (Lindenbaum, Chakraborty, and Elias 1985; Levine and others 1987; Caldwell 1979). In the words of Peter Adamson (1988), "Education erodes resignation and substitutes for it a degree of confidence, an awareness of choice, a belief that decisions can be made, circumstances changed, life improved." Using qualitative research techniques, Griffiths (1988) has identified some of the mechanisms through which maternal confidence and self-esteem affect child health. Her research in Cameroon, India, and Indonesia has demonstrated that mothers with higher self-esteem take a more assertive role in their child's feeding—they introduce weaning foods at the appropriate age, they take swifter action when a child is sick, and they persist in feeding even when a child refuses. Not surprisingly, more confident mothers have better nourished children.

If education is in fact a proxy for some intervening variable such as self-confidence or autonomy, anything that undermines confidence will affect child health. Acts of violence and society's tacit acceptance of them stand as constant reminders to women of their low worth. Where women's confidence and status are critical to achieving a development goal—such as improving child survival—violence, or the fear of it, will remain a powerful obstacle to progress.

New empirical data also link abuse of women by their husbands to the nutritional status of their children. In a census study of married women in three villages in rural Karnataka, India, qualitative and quantitative data indicated that inadequate payment of dowries and men's consumption of alcohol were the single greatest predictors of whether a wife would be beaten (Rao and Bloch 1993). The children of women who were beaten were more malnourished and received less food than other equivalent children, a result the authors suggest may stem from the effects of wife beating on women's bargaining position in marriage.

6. Steps toward eliminating violence against women

Violence against women is an extremely complex phenomenon, deeply rooted in gender-based power relations, sexuality, self-identity, and social institutions. Any strategy to eliminate gender violence must therefore confront the underlying cultural beliefs and social structures that perpetuate it. To be effective, such a strategy would have to draw on a wide range of expertise and resources, both governmental and nongovernmental.

Our understanding of the exact causes of gender violence still needs refining. But the results of several recent cross-cultural studies on family violence and rape reinforce the feminist contention that hierarchical gender relations—perpetuated through gender socialization and socioeconomic inequalities—play an integral role in violence against women (box 4). Using complex statistics and coded ethnographic data from 90 societies throughout the world, Levinson (1989) identified four factors that, taken together, are strong predictors of the prevalence of violence against women in a society. These factors are economic inequality between men and women, a pattern of using physical violence to resolve conflict, male authority and control of decisionmaking in the home, and divorce restrictions for women. The study suggests that economic inequality for women is the strongest factor, reinforced by male control in the family and a woman's inability to divorce.

These findings reinforce the feminist view that violence against women is not an inherent part of "maleness" but a function of socially constructed norms of acceptable behavior. As Cheryl Bernard, Director of Austria's Ludwig Boltzmann Institute of Politics, notes:

> Violence against women in the family takes place because the perpetrators feel, and their environment encourages them to feel, that this is an acceptable exercise of male prerogative, a legitimate and appropriate way to relieve their own tension in conditions of stress, to sanction

female behavior...or just to enjoy a feeling of supremacy. (Bernard 1986, p. 26)

Indeed, in many societies women are defined as inferior and the right to dominate them is considered an essential aspect of being male. A strategy to prevent violence must therefore begin by dismantling these cultural beliefs and deconstructing notions of masculinity that promote aggressive sexual behavior and domination of women. To the extent that male sexual behavior is "predatory" in certain cultures, it is not because male

---

Box 4 Correlates of gender violence in cross-cultural studies

Predictive of high violence

1. Violent interpersonal conflict resolution[a, c]
2. Economic inequality between men and women[c]
3. Masculine ideal of male dominance, toughness, honor[a, b]
4. Male economic and decisionmaking authority in the family[c]

Predictive of low violence

1. Female power outside the home[a, b, c]
2. Active community intervention in violence[b, c]
3. Presence of all-female work or solidarity groups[b, c]
4. Sanctuary from violence (shelters, friends, family)[b]

---

a. Sanday 1981.
b. Counts, Brown, and Campbell 1992.
c. Levinson 1989.

"sexuality" is aggressive, but because sexuality is used to express power relations based on gender. Thus any effort to eradicate violence must also address the underlying power dimensions.

Clearly, any systematic effort to root out violence must be multidimensional, drawing on the expertise and resources of many sectors, both governmental and nongovernmental. Although the response of the health sector is clearly important, a strategy that seeks to go beyond treating "the symptoms" of abuse must focus on eliminating the attitudes and beliefs that legitimize violence and justify male control of female behavior. And it must improve women's access to power and resources so as to give them realistic alternatives to staying in abusive relationships. As JoAnne Leslie, codirector of the Los Angeles-based Pacific Institute for Women's Health, observes: "To the extent that more education, higher incomes, occupations outside of the home, access to credit etc. empower women and enhance their self esteem, these may prove much more effective in reducing the morbidity and mortality associated with domestic violence, than more direct health sector intervention" (1992, p. 26).

A strategy to prevent violence must also promote nonviolent means to resolve conflict (between all members of society—men, boys, family members). Passing laws to criminalize violence within family relationships—in the same way that societies criminalize violence between strangers—is an important way to redefine the frontiers of acceptable behavior. Using violence to resolve conflicts is a learned behavior—children are exposed to violence by their parents' behavior in their homes and through television, film, and videos. Levinson's study suggests that violence against women is particularly prevalent in societies in which the use of force to resolve interpersonal conflicts is condoned.

This policy section recommends actions involving a broad range of actors. Appendix A outlines a comprehensive program designed to confront and eliminate violence against women, which includes both long-term actions to prevent future violence and shorter-term responses to victims' needs. The reader may wish to review the appendix before reading further. The section that follows explores some of the interventions and approaches that have been tried in different parts of the world, to give a sense of the innovative programming that is beginning to evolve.

Unlike for many health and development issues, the most important step that can be taken to combat violence is fairly clear: support the nascent initiatives already under way. Some of these are at the governmental level (see box 5 for examples), but most represent the untiring efforts of autonomous women's organizations that have pushed this issue forward despite local and national resistance. To be effective, work to combat violence must be site-specific, emerging from the cultural and political realities of each country. A wealth of well-organized NGOs are already working throughout the developing world on many of the programs outlined below. A recent directory published by ISIS International (1990) lists 379 separate organizations working on gender violence issues in Latin America alone. These groups, which function with little outside support, could easily be strengthened with a minimal investment of resources.

Justice system reform

The gross inadequacy of most laws in protecting victims or sanctioning violent perpetrators has made legal reform an important priority for many groups working on violence against women. Clearly, amending laws on paper is not enough to ensure change, but strong laws can be a considerable asset in helping women protect themselves from violence. Three critical tasks in legal reform are changing laws that keep women trapped in abusive relationships, removing barriers to prosecution, and eliminating aspects of the law that are prejudicial to women.

A number of laws have worked to trap women in relationships. Article 114 of Guatemala's Civil Code, for example, grants a woman's husband the right to prohibit her from working outside the home; among other things, this drastically limits a woman's ability to gain the financial independence needed to escape an abusive relationship (Garcia 1992). In Ecuador, until a 1989 legal reform, a husband had the right to force his wife to live with him no matter how abusive he may have been (Ponce, Palan, and Jacome 1992). And in Chile divorce is illegal for any reason, even in cases of extreme violence (Valdez 1992). Such laws put women living in violent relationships at substantial risk.

Laws in other countries make it almost impossible to prosecute violence against women, especially violence perpetrated by an intimate partner. In Pakistan, for example, four male Muslim witnesses must testify before a man can be convicted and subjected to the *hadd* punishment (the most severe) for rape (Human Rights Watch 1992). It is extremely difficult in Pakistan to get any conviction of rape, even for the lesser *tazir* penalty (public flogging, rigorous imprisonment, or fines), because the Law of Evidence considers women "incompetent" as witnesses in cases of rape and grants their testimony only the status of corroborative evidence. In 1979 Pakistan passed the *hudood* ordinance, which made all forms of sex outside marriage—including fornication and adultery—crimes against the state. Women who have failed to meet Pakistan's high standard of proof for rape have themselves been thrown in jail for adultery or fornication based on their admission of intercourse. Human rights activists estimate that up to 1,500 Pakistani women are in prison awaiting trial for *hudood* violations (Human Rights Watch 1992).

Rape laws that are prejudicial against women are not uncommon. The definition of rape is extremely narrow in most countries, and the law and judicial systems often treat rape as a crime against public morality, family honor, or—as in African customary law—property, rather than as a crime against the woman. In cases of sexual violence the justice system is almost universally biased against women who are not virgins. In some Latin American countries—for example, Brazil, Costa Rica, Ecuador, and Guatemala—the law defines certain sexual offenses as crimes only if they are committed against "honest"—that is, virginal—women or girls. Laws in Chile and Guatemala specifically exonerate a man who agrees to marry the girl he has raped; his marriage to the victim is perceived as restoring her honor and that of her family (Garcia 1992; Valdez 1992).

In addition, in the vast majority of countries the law does not recognize marital rape or domestic violence. Although most legal systems have laws against assault, these provisions are often difficult to use to convict an intimate partner. In Latin America the definition of assault often requires a finding of injury sufficient to incapacitate the victim for a set number of days (frequently a week or more). Normally, such findings must be made by an official forensic doctor, who evaluates whether the incident meets the legal definition of injury, or *lesion*. But because incapacitation is usually framed in terms of inability to work, and because work is seen as employment outside the home, a woman's injury may not be interpreted as a *lesion,* regardless of the physical or mental health consequences it may have for her.

Similar distinctions hold in India, where assaults that do not cause "grievous harm" are "noncognizable" offenses— that is, the police can take no action without first seeking a warrant from a magistrate. "Grievous harm" includes only certain types of permanent injuries, such as emasculation, loss of sight or hearing, or permanent

---

Box 5 Government initiatives against gender-based violence

In February 1991 the government of *Canada* announced a new four-year Family Violence Initiative, a "call to action" intended to mobilize community action, strengthen Canada's legal framework, establish services on Indian reserves and in Inuit communities, develop resources to help victims and stop offenders, and provide housing for abused women and their children (Government of Canada 1991).

In 1991 *Chile's* Congress created El Servicio Nacional de la Mujer (SERNAM) to advance the rights and opportunities of Chilean women. SERNAM has proposed a program to prevent family violence by promoting legal reform to criminalize domestic violence, documenting the dimensions of the problem, organizing community awareness campaigns to change public consciousness, and opening crisis centers to provide legal and psychological support (Servicio Nacional de la Mujer 1991).

Brazil's new constitution, enacted in 1988, contains the following provision: The states should assist the family, in the person of each of its members, and should create mechanisms so as to impede violence in the sphere of its relationships (Americas Watch 1991). And *Colombia's* 1989 constitution states that "any form of violence within the family is considered destructive to its harmony and unity and will be sanctioned by law" (ISIS International 1993).

In March 1990 the prime minister of *Australia* established the Commonwealth/State National Committee on Violence Against Women (NCVAW) with a three-year budget of $1.35 million. The NCVAW initiates research, coordinates the development of policy, programs, legislation, and law enforcement on a national level, and conducts and coordinates community education on violence against women. Among the committee's founding principles: "women have a fundamental right to be safe," and "men must be held completely responsible for their violence" (NCVAW 1991).

In 1992 Bolivia's National Council for Solidarity and Social Development opened an Office of Battered Women, which runs a halfway house where women can seek refuge and receive medical treatment and counseling. "We are absolutely new at dealing with this," said Maria Luisa Palacios, national director of the Social Welfare Agency. "We're looking for other women's groups to help us understand how to handle this problem" (Nash 1992).

Ecuador's National Development Plan for 1988-92 included, for the first time, an entire chapter on improving the situation of women. And in 1991 the government body in charge of women's affairs (DINAMU) added a new line of action—consciousness-raising and action against violence against women. DINAMU has opened a legal services office and a battered women's shelter, but the effectiveness of these state services for women has so far been limited (Ponce, Palan, and Jacome 1992).

---

disfigurement of the face (Articles 319-26 of the Indian Penal Code; Agnes 1988).

In the legal systems of many countries the burden of proof and the penalties for violence against women are biased against intimate assaults. Article 276 of the Bolivian Penal Code, for example, states that *lesions* caused by a husband are punishable only if they incapacitate a woman for more than 30 days (Rosenberg 1992). In Peru the stiffest sentence possible for wife abuse is 30 days of community service. Lawyers who represent battered women say that, in practice, even this minimal penalty is rarely enforced (Kirk 1993).

The forensic medicine system in Latin America and parts of Asia complicates the prospects of rape convictions. In most countries only government-employed forensic doctors are authorized to collect evidence on rape admissible in court. These physicians are generally located only in large cities, and their offices are closed in the evenings and on weekends. (In Lima, Peru, where there are only five forensic doctors, a rural woman raped on a Thursday night might have to travel all day by bus and then wait two days before she could be examined.) Moreover, forensic doctors seldom have specialized training in rape or domestic violence, and they routinely omit from their reports information crucial to establishing the commission of a crime (Kirk 1993).

In recent years some countries have made significant strides toward improving written laws relating to violence against women. In July 1991 Mexico revised its rape law in several important ways. It redefined rape as "a crime against a person's freedom" (rather than against morality), expanded the definition of rape to include anal, oral, and vaginal penetration, increased the sentence for rapists, eliminated a provision allowing a man who rapes a minor to avoid prosecution if he agrees to marry her, and required judges to hand down a decision regarding access to an abortion within five working days (*Women's World* 1991-92).

Steps toward reform have also been taken in the Philippines. In 1993 a coalition of 14 women's groups developed and got introduced in Congress a progressive rape law that incorporates an expanded definition of rape, redefines rape as a crime against the person (and not her chastity), makes marital rape illegal, recognizes "physical or verbal resistance in any degree...as prima facie evidence of lack of consent," disallows information on the sexual history of the woman to prejudice her claim, and establishes a woman's right to a closed-door court hearing (Women's Legal Bureau 1992).

A growing number of governments, including some in the developing world (the Bahamas, Barbados, Belize, Malaysia, Puerto Rico), have passed laws or reformed their penal codes to criminalize domestic violence. And a substantial number of countries—including Argentina,

Bolivia, Brazil, Chile, Colombia, Ecuador, Peru, and Venezuela—have bills under consideration (ISIS International 1993). Often such laws criminalize psychological as well as physical violence and provide for orders of protection— legally binding court orders that prohibit one person from abusing another. Under the most progressive statutes judges can require a man to leave his home, establish temporary custody and visitation arrangements for children, make the husband pay financial support, forbid telephone threats and harassment, and order the batterer to attend counseling. Many women prefer protection orders to criminal prosecution because they do not want their abuser jailed or wish to avoid the trauma and expense of a trial.

The effectiveness of protection orders depends largely on how well they are enforced. Too often, protection orders become meaningless pieces of paper because police and judges refuse to impose the penalties for noncompliance. Where orders are enforced rigorously, however, they can offer a substantial subset of women considerable protection, and make it possible for them and their children to stay at home. Of course, for some men—those who are especially violent, jealous, and obsessive—the orders are essentially useless; the only way to protect their partners is to incarcerate the abuser.

Elsewhere, governments have passed laws against particular types of violence common in their countries. The Indian government has passed a law against "Eve teasing," the sexual and physical harassment of girls and women in public. Both India and Pakistan have passed laws against dowry harassment, and Bangladesh has outlawed acid throwing. None of these laws is widely enforced, however (Heise 1989). Colombia's congress is considering a law that would make *secuestro* (the confinement or isolation) of a wife by a husband a crime. The law was proposed in response to the growing trend among Colombian men to lock up their wives to prevent infidelity (Maridos Secuestradores 1992).

As with protection orders, such laws are only as good as their enforcement, and it is in implementation that the legal response to violence most notably fails. Nonetheless, important initiatives have been taken in recent years to improve the response of the justice system to gender-based violence (box 6). Perhaps the best known has been the creation of women-only police stations, an innovation that has spread from Brazil to Colombia, Uruguay, Peru, Costa Rica, and Argentina.[17] Data from Brazil's special police stations show that women-only units have greatly facilitated the reporting of abuse. In Sao Paulo, for example, reported rape cases went from 67 in 1985, before the women's police stations were opened, to 841 in 1990. Sao Paulo has 96 of the country's 125 women's police stations; these registered 79,000 of the national total of 205,000 crimes against women reported between July 1991 and August 1992, suggesting that the number of reported cases would be much higher if women's police stations were more widely available in other states (Dimenstein 1992).

Although the women's police stations are an important innovation, they have also had problems. Many stations have been overrun with women seeking assistance that the stations do not provide: counseling, legal advice, and help with state bureaucracies. The original plans to assign social workers and lawyers to each station have not materialized. The female police officers assigned to these stations become easily demoralized because their male peers do not consider their job "real police work." Moreover, observers have learned that, without training, female officers are not necessarily more sensitive to women's needs than their male colleagues (although women have proven more open and responsive to training). Finally, the special stations have not increased the rate of prosecution because at higher levels the justice system remains unchanged. Nonetheless, because the stations encourage women to come forward, they have helped deter violence among men who worry about being reported to the police.

In industrial countries the most recent innovation in combating violence against women has been "coordinated community intervention." This strategy brings together the policymakers concerned—from battered women's groups, law enforcement agencies, the justice system, batterer treatment programs, and other relevant groups—in regular meetings to develop a coordinated response to domestic violence. Once policies are developed, lower-level representatives are assigned to meet regularly to oversee their implementation. Roughly 75 to 100 communities in the United States have adopted this model. The strategy includes several key elements. There are written policies about how each agency should respond and agreements on coordination and sharing data. A paid coordinator manages the task force and oversees the processing of cases. Victims' advocates are trained to help battered women negotiate the court system and other social service agencies, and training is also given to all relevant staff on the dynamics of abuse and related policies. Local shelters or safe homes are provided, as are batterer treatment programs. And there is active monitoring—preferably by an autonomous women's group—to ensure that each agency carries out its policy and coordinates properly with other actors. Similar community intervention strategies are being implemented in Canadian cities (Heise and Chapman 1992).

Health care system reform

The health care system is well placed to identify and refer victims of violence. It is the only public institution likely to interact with all women at some point in their lives—as they seek contraception, give birth, or seek care for their children. Experience has shown that this access is important.

Box 6 Innovative justice system reform projects

In the *United States* feminist lawyers organized the Judicial Education Program to Promote Equality for Women and Men in the Courts (Heise and Chapman 1992). This program has succeeded in getting more than half the states to form "gender-bias" task forces to detect and attack sexism in the courts. The task forces, made up of judges and community representatives, have uncovered devastating testimony by victims of abuse about their mistreatment in the courts and have prompted the recall of some judges and increased training for judges and prosecutors. The Asia Pacific Forum on Women, Law, and Development is undertaking a similar project that is analyzing the laws in seven Asian countries (Fernando 1993).

In Harare, *Zimbabwe,* the Musassa Project works with local police and prosecutors to sensitize them to issues of domestic violence and rape. Commenting on their work, the organizers observe that "the specifics of an educational strategy aimed to justice system professionals must be very carefully devised. In many cases, credibility must be ensured by involving a legal professional in the education process, and the content must be highly dependable and informed. Another effective technique is to facilitate a workshop with one part of the legal system acting as host to another (police hosting prosecutors, for example)" (Stewart 1992).

In *Costa Rica,* El Instituto Legal de los Naciones Unidas y Desarollo (ILANUD) offers gender sensitivity training, emphasizing violence against women, to prosecutors, judges, lawyers, and other professionals. In 1992 the project conducted 32 workshops throughout Latin America (Facio 1993).

In *Malaysia* five organizations joined forces at the end of 1984 to form the Joint Action Group Against Violence Against Women (JAG). JAG organized a major media campaign against rape, initiated dialogue with the police and the medical profession, and successfully lobbied for the creation of women-only rape teams on the police force. The Health Ministry agreed in 1987 to set up one-stop crisis centers in all hospitals, staffed by medical personnel and trained volunteers from local women's organizations. The centers have not yet been established, however (APDC 1989).

Even in countries with a strong movement against violence, many abused women never choose to call the police or a crisis hot line, the two most widely developed sources for referral. Advocates in Connecticut, for example, estimate that only 10 percent of battered women living in that state ever come in contact with its extensive network of legal advocates, shelters, and crisis centers. This may be in large part because the system relies primarily on the police and crisis hot lines to inform victims about the services available (Heise and Chapman 1992). In politically repressive countries, the likelihood of the police serving as an adequate referral system is even less realistic.[18]

Women who are unable or unwilling to seek help from the police or other government authorities may nonetheless admit abuse when questioned gently and in private by a supportive health care provider. Providers have found that, contrary to their expectations, women are willing to admit abuse when questioned directly and non-judgmentally. For example, when Planned Parenthood of Houston and Southeast Texas added four abuse assessment questions to its standard intake form, 8.2 percent of women identified themselves as physically abused. When a provider asked the same questions in person, 29 percent of women reported abuse (Bullock and others 1989). Researchers have found that three to four simple questions are generally enough to screen for physical and sexual abuse (see box 7 for examples). Questions should be asked in person and in private, and the questioner should make sure that the potential abuser is not present to avoid putting the woman at additional risk.

Some who have implemented programs to screen for abuse at prenatal care clinics and emergency rooms note that asking itself can be an important intervention. "It is my impression that some women have been waiting their whole lives for someone to ask," notes Dr. Ana Flavia d'Oliveira (1993), a Brazilian public health physician who initiated an abuse screening program among her prenatal care patients. Providers can emphasize to a woman that no one deserves to be beaten or raped, and help her think through options for protecting herself (for example, seeking safety at a friend's house). In urban areas providers can refer women to a growing number of services for legal or psychological support (see the section below on assisting victims). Even where no external support exists, having a sympathetic individual acknowledge and denounce the violence in a woman's life offers relief from isolation and self-blame.

Providers can also help a woman better assess the degree of danger that her abuser poses to her and her children. In the United States, for example, researchers have developed a list of warning signs that indicate that a woman is at substantially increased risk of homicide or serious injury. The list includes the following (see appendix D for a complete danger assessment):

- Has the violence escalated over the past year?
- Is there a gun in the house?
- Has he threatened to kill you?
- Has your partner forced you into sex when you did not want it?
- Is your partner violent outside the home?
- Is your partner drunk every day or almost every day?

Box 7 Abuse assessment screen

1. Have you ever been emotionally or physically abused by your partner or someone important to you?

   YES   NO

2. Within the last year, have you been hit, slapped, kicked, or otherwise physically hurt by someone?

   YES   NO

   If yes, by whom _____

   Number of times _____

3. Since you've been pregnant, have you been hit, slapped, kicked, or otherwise physically hurt by someone?

   YES   NO

   If yes, by whom _____

   Number of times _____

   Mark the area of injury on the body map [map provided]

4. Within the last year, has anyone forced you to have sexual activities?

   YES   NO

   If yes, who _____

   Number of times _____

5. Are you afraid of your partner or anyone you listed above?

   YES   NO

Note: Developed by the Nursing Research Consortium on Violence and Abuse, United States.
Source: Parker and others 1993.

- Has your partner ever beaten you while you were pregnant?

Statistical analysis shows that women who answer yes to a cluster of these questions are at higher risk of being fatally wounded by their partner. By administering this simple danger assessment checklist, providers can help women evaluate their situation and take precautionary measures. Although a checklist along precisely these lines may not be appropriate in settings outside the United States, the analysis required to derive such indicators is straightforward and a list appropriate to any area could easily be developed.

Despite the potentially critical role of health care professionals, evidence indicates that few providers identify and respond appropriately to victims of abuse (Warshaw 1989). In evaluating 481 medical records of women seeking aid for injuries at a major U.S. urban emergency room, physicians identified only 2.8 percent as battered. But closer examination of the records showed that 16 percent of the women had injuries considered probably or highly suggestive of abuse and almost 10 percent could be positively identified as battered. Another 15 percent had trauma histories suggesting battering (Stark and others 1981). This means that emergency room staff identified only about one in eight battered women who passed through their service.

In Alexandra Township, South Africa, a rapidly urbanizing community near the heart of Johannesburg, a similar retrospective study reviewed the charts of 398 women presenting with a history of assault to the Casualty Department of Alexandra Health Clinic during October and November 1991. The survey found that providers failed to record the identity of the perpetrator in 78 percent of cases; charts included such agent-less descriptions as "chopped with an axe" or "stabbed with a knife." Charts providing more complete information include the following cases:

- A 35-year-old woman was kicked and stabbed with a screwdriver by her boyfriend. On physical examination, she had suprapubic tenderness, laceration of the labia minora, and swelling on her forehead.
- A 32-year-old woman was assaulted and raped by her husband. When she reported the incident to the local traditional healer, he also raped her.
- A 32-year-old woman who was being assaulted by her husband left the house to seek help from her relatives. On her way, she was raped by three men.
- A 15-year-old, married and six months pregnant, was raped by a neighbor. Her husband was away, working on a contract job in one of the homelands.

Studies show that with proper training and protocols,

however, health care facilities can greatly improve their staff's sensitivity to gender-based abuse (see appendix D for information on protocols). After the emergency department of the Medical College of Pennsylvania introduced training and protocols, the share of female trauma patients found to be battered increased more than fivefold, from 5.6 percent to 30 percent (McCleer and Anwar 1989). Similarly, prenatal care providers who received training through a program funded by the March of Dimes significantly increased their rate of screening for abuse. After six months 75 percent of program directors reported that they had implemented abuse screening, up from zero before training (Helton, McFarlane, and Anderson 1987).

Despite their usefulness, protocols and training are still rare in the United States. Only 20 percent of emergency departments in Massachusetts—one of the better-organized states—had a written protocol for domestic violence in 1991 (Isaac and Sanchez 1992). That same year, however, two important initiatives were launched that should improve the health sector's involvement in the issue of violence. First, the American Medical Association (AMA) initiated a major campaign to educate physicians and the public about family violence and devoted an entire issue of its prestigious *Journal of the American Medical Association* to the theme. Second, the U.S. Joint Commission on Hospital Accreditation included emergency room protocols and training on family violence among the criteria used to evaluate hospitals for accreditation (Heise and Chapman 1992). This policy change should encourage more active screening and referral of abuse victims. A new project sponsored by the Family Violence Prevention Fund, a private, nonprofit group in San Francisco, and the Pennsylvania Coalition Against Domestic Violence seeks to help institutionalize the new hospital accreditation standards by developing model protocols, training programs, and dissemination strategies that can be applied throughout the country (Family Violence Prevention Fund 1993).

Training providers is essential not only to increase referral rates, but to ensure that victims are not revictimized by the health care system. Victims of rape and domestic assault frequently report being humiliated and degraded by the very providers who are supposed to help them (Kirk 1993). Providers who fail to collect and record evidence properly in rape and assault cases can jeopardize any legal cases that a victim might bring. And providers ignorant of violence and its sequelae can exacerbate the consequences for women by labeling them hypochondriacs or by treating them for nonexistent mental illnesses. Research from the United States shows that emergency room doctors are more likely to prescribe tranquilizers and pain medication to battered women than to trauma victims who are not battered (Stark, Flitcraft, and Frazier 1979). By deadening the pain and clouding judgment, tranquilizers can prolong the battering relationship and make it more difficult for women to assess their options or take action to protect themselves. It is widely acknowledged that Valium and other tranquilizers are overprescribed by the medical profession in the developing world as well (Busto 1991).

The issue of violence can and should be incorporated into the training of community health workers as well as professional staff. Project workers report that such issues as domestic violence and men's alcoholism arise spontaneously during health promoter meetings, especially in all-female groups. Increasingly, NGO-sponsored projects are incorporating themes on gender violence and women's status into training materials for health promoters. The Women's Program of Uraco Pueblo in Honduras, for example, includes socio-dramas, discussions, and role playing on domestic violence and sexual harassment in its health promoter training; promoters regularly hold community meetings on domestic violence, inviting lawyers to offer women legal advice and holding joint meetings with husbands and other men from the village (Maher, personal communication, 1993). And female health workers in the SARTHI project in Gujurat, India, consider offering individual and community support to victims of violence an integral part of their job. Health promoters have accompanied women to the police station to register complaints and worked with family members to marshal support for women's decisions to take action against an abusive husband. Project organizer Renu Khanna notes that the women themselves defined violence as a priority; SARTHI merely supported their leadership on the issue (Khanna, personal communication, 1992).

On the international front tentative progress has also been made toward recognizing violence as an obstacle to women's health and development. In 1991 the Pan-American Health Organization (PAHO) sponsored a conference in Managua entitled "Violence against Women: A Problem of Public Health" (OPS 1992). Colombia's Ministry of Health issued an action agenda for women's health which included a program on "Prevention of Abuse and Attention to Victims of Violence." And the United Nations Fund for Women (UNIFEM) published "Battered Dreams: Violence against Women as an Obstacle to Development" (Carrillo 1992). But the World Health Organization has no program or policy related to gender-based violence. In fact, in planning World Health Day 1993—whose theme was Injury and Violence Prevention— officials included no mention of violence against women until women's health advocates persuaded them to do so.

Prevention programs

Although violence is in theory largely preventable, few preventive programs have been undertaken on a wide scale.[19] Among those programs that do exist, many focus on helping adolescents and young children learn non-violent ways to resolve conflict (box 8). Some concentrate on developing self-esteem and the ability to express emotions in constructive, nonviolent ways. Others work to challenge the gender stereotypes and notions of male prerogative perpetuated in the media and in the culture at large. Programs in some schools encourage children to disclose to an adult unwanted touching by strangers or family members. And on college campuses consciousness-raising programs are being developed to combat acquaintance rape.

Much of the public education and media work by the women's movement can also be loosely classed as prevention work, although more effort has been directed at reaching potential victims than at changing men's attitudes. Women's groups have held hundreds of workshops and produced thousands of pamphlets, comic books, and other consciousness-raising materials to give women basic information about their rights. Although few of these materials have been evaluated, they have clearly been useful in initiating dialogue on this often taboo subject (Zurutuza 1993). Several developing countries, among them Ecuador and Peru, have sponsored national media campaigns to sensitize the public to issues concerning rape and domestic violence (Zurutuza 1993). The Family Violence Prevention Fund in San Francisco is trying to take media-based prevention a step further by doing sophisticated market research to craft messages aimed at changing public attitudes toward violence. This effort represents the first time that the media techniques successfully used to change drinking and smoking behavior in the United States will be applied to domestic violence.

In recent years justice system intervention (arrest, prosecution) has been advanced in the United States and Canada as a tool to prevent future violence among already violent men. Until the late 1970s the traditional response by police to domestic calls (when they responded at all) was to walk the abuser around the block, using arrest only as a last resort. This changed dramatically in the United States during the 1980s as police departments—responding to pressure from advocates for battered women, fear of liability suits, and a flurry of new mandatory arrest laws—began to arrest offenders for intimate assaults.[20] Also prompting the shift in social policy were research results from Minneapolis, published in 1984, suggesting that, compared with separating couples or advising them to get help, arrest cut in half the risk of future assaults over a six-month follow-up period (Sherman and Berk 1984). These findings were widely publicized by advocates seeking to criminalize wife assault and thus end the double standard of policing for private and public violence.

But recent replication studies have called into question the results of the Minneapolis experiment (Schmidt and Sherman 1993). Of five studies, only two (Colorado Springs and Miami) found even weak support for the greater efficacy of arrest compared with other police interventions. Detailed analysis reveals that the effect of arrest varies with characteristics of the perpetrator. When the perpetrator is married or employed, or both, arrest reduces recidivism, but for unemployed and unattached perpetrators, arrest actually increased abuse in some cities. Some have interpreted employment and marriage as measures of "social embeddedness," arguing that arrest deters men who have more to lose (Sherman and Smith 1992). But it is equally plausible that employment is a surrogate for other factors not measured, such as education, self-esteem, and socioeconomic standing. Teasing out the exact nature and causes of the differential effect will require further analysis and research.[21]

This is not to say that arrest serves no useful purpose in domestic violence cases, but only that it may not, on average, reduce recidivism more effectively than other possible police interventions. In fact, advocates' original objective in promoting arrest was not to deter future violence, but to interrupt current abuse and to ensure women's equal protection under the law (Stark 1993). The questionable ability of arrest to deter intimate assaults makes it no less effective than for other crimes: the literature on juvenile delinquency and on general criminology offers little empirical or theoretical support for arrest deterring juvenile or adult offenders (Gelles 1993). It may also be that arrest alone is not enough. A study by Steinman (1989) found that arrest in isolation from other criminal justice sanctions produced greater subsequent violence. But when part of an integrated justice system response that included prosecution and court-mandated treatment, arrests offered significant protection from further abuse.

Elsewhere in the world women have begun to organize to prevent genital mutilation and other traditional practices harmful to women and girls. In 1984, at a World Health

---

Box 8 Initiatives to prevent gender-based violence

In *Kingston, Jamaica,* three groups use popular theater for prevention education on gender violence. The artistic collective Sistern uses interactive workshops and street theater to prompt discussions on issues of domestic violence and rape. The Women's Media Watch protests violence and objectionable portrayals of women in the media and uses theater work with young people to help them grapple with complex questions relating to sexuality and sexual violence. Teens in Action, a community group formed after the brutal rape and murder of a young girl, performs drama to encourage critical reflection in their neighborhood on issues of sexuality, male-female relationships, and rape (Popular Education Research Group 1992).

In *Ontario, Canada,* the Ministry of Education's Violence Prevention Initiative schools children in the three "R's" plus one: relationships. The program includes a school-based family violence prevention curriculum tested in the schools in 1991-92, a Handbook for the Prevention of Family Violence developed with the input of more than 60 professionals, and a family violence training program for school personnel. The project has published and distributed thousands of pamphlets and storybooks, sponsored theater groups, organized parent-teacher days, and worked with schools, the police, medical staff, shelter workers, and social service agencies to make them more aware of the issue (Etue 1991).

In *Brooklyn, New York,* the Anti-Violence Education Project uses self-defense training as an entree for discussing violence prevention with children in the public schools. The project holds weekly sessions to teach children self-defense and nonviolent ways to resolve conflict. It draws analogies between relationship strategies and the philosophy of karate; it teaches that the martial arts do not condone violence, but instead that the true master is the one who can use the least force to achieve his or her ends. It also teaches children to look critically at how the media misrepresent the martial arts through the depiction of such pseudo-heros as Bruce Lee (Ellman 1993).

Education Wife Assault (EWA) in *Toronto, Ontario,* works with immigrant and refugee women to help them develop culturally appropriate violence prevention campaigns for their community. The EWA holds "skill shops" that give women leaders the skills they need to develop their own culturally specific programs against domestic violence. It then provides technical support to the women carrying out the campaigns. The EWA's staff also lend emotional support to women organizers to help them overcome the isolation and the backlash often directed at women working against domestic violence because of perceptions that they are threatening community and cultural cohesiveness (Center for Women's Global Leadership 1992).

Organization–sponsored conference in Dakar, Senegal, 22 national committees working to eradicate genital mutilation joined to form the Inter-African Committee on Traditional Practices Affecting the Health of Women and Children. In the words of Berhane Ras Work, the committee's president, "female circumcision is a clear example of social violence which women have to bear in silence as a price for marriage and social identity" (Heise 1993, p. 180).

In 1990, at a conference in Addis Ababa, Ethiopia, on "Traditional Practices Affecting the Health of Women and Children: How Far Forward?," African delegates voted to support laws to ban female genital mutilation and punish those who carry out the practice. The first United Nations Human Rights Seminar on Traditional Practices—held in Ouagadougou, Burkina Faso, in May 1991—recommended using legislation, education, and such means as street theater and community organizing to end harmful practices (Dorkenoo and Scilla 1992). African women living in Europe, Canada, and the United States have also begun to organize to combat the practice among immigrant and refugee populations (Hedley and Dorkenoo 1992).

Programs to assist victims

In the industrial world rape crisis centers and battered women's shelters have been the cornerstone of programs to assist abuse victims. A typical rape crisis center supports a 24-hour hot line, community education programs, staff or volunteers who accompany raped women to the hospital and police station, training for health and justice professionals, and ongoing counseling or support groups for victims. Shelters provide emergency housing for women and children for up to several months. They also provide hot lines, support groups for residents, community education programs, basic child care, and women's advocates who help residents negotiate the legal system and social service bureaucracies. Some better-funded shelters provide legal assistance and job training, and employ staff who carry out training and institutional reform efforts to reduce violence against women (Heise and Chapman 1992).

Since the early 1980s shelters and women's crisis centers have sprung up in many developing countries too. At least 40 developing countries now have at least a handful of NGOs that assist victims of violence. Some countries have both specialized rape crisis centers and separate services for battered women; others have one or more all-purpose crisis centers to which female victims of any kind of gender violence can go for services. Because of the expense of maintaining shelters, many developing country NGOs have decided not to open any, and instead to concentrate their limited resources on self-help support groups, legal services, counseling, and institutional reform. Some women's organizations have also rejected the shelter model because they see it as reinforcing dependency rather than promoting networking and problem solving (Carcedo, personal communication, 1993).

A few governments, especially at the municipal level, have also begun to provide services for battered women and rape victims. In 1989 the Mexican government, for example, created specialized agencies under the District Attorney's office for the reporting of sexual violence. These agencies aim to provide legal, medical, and psychological care to survivors in a sensitive and confidential atmosphere. New legislation has been introduced to provide long-term support for the five specialized agencies in Mexico City and for agencies in all 31 state capitals (*Women's World* 1991-92). Likewise, Peru's Ministry of Health is seeking low-cost ways to shelter female victims of violence. The Director of Mental Health, Mariano Querol, recently visited the United States to investigate models for assisting victims in sparsely populated rural areas (Querol, personal communication, 1992).

In both the industrial and the developing world, support groups play an integral role in healing and consciousness-raising. As Lucrecia Oller, coordinator of the Violence Prevention Program at Lugar de Mujer in Buenos Aires, Argentina, observes:

> The group becomes a space where the abused woman can begin to visualize her recuperation. She has ongoing communication with women who have been working at this for a long time, and who share what they've gone through with her. Under these circumstances, the first tangible tool she receives from the group is hope; she sees that others have been able to free themselves, and begins to think that perhaps she can too. (Popular Education Research Group 1992, p. 11)

Support groups help abused women begin to live fuller, more productive lives. They play a critical role even for women unable or unwilling to leave an abusive partner, by helping them to stop blaming themselves, by reducing their isolation, and by providing a springboard for social activism. The role of social support in reducing stress reactions has also been well documented (van der Kolk 1988; Rachley 1990). As Lucrecia Oller observes, "to feel heard and understood is to begin to feel human" (Popular Education Research Group 1992, p. 11).

Support can also help women escape future violence. A recent evaluation by the Costa Rican women's organization CEFEMINA found that 60 percent of the abused women who attended its support groups were able to achieve a violence-free life within six months—most by leaving the

g less than $20,000 a year to reach
, or roughly $50 per woman served,
program is highly cost-effective
communication, 1993).
s are also used to assist victims of
adolescent sexual abuse. As part of its
vention project, for example, the Costa
er y Crecer trains professionals in three
communit...—teachers, therapists, social workers—to run
self-help support groups for victims of sexual abuse. The
project provides three months of training and guidelines
on conducting a 16-session support group. Ser y Crecer
also teaches local leaders from these same professional
communities to identify and refer victims of abuse, and
trains other professionals as "prevention experts" to
conduct prevention education in their communities. A
nurse, for example, might be trained to give talks to
parents waiting in a doctor's office (Batres, personal
communication, 1993).

Elsewhere in the world, communities are developing
their own ways to sanction perpetrators and assist abuse
victims, often by increasing the "social cost" of violent
behavior through public confrontation and humiliation.
Among the Garifuna, an Afro-Indian population inhabiting
the Caribbean coast of Belize, for example, women
surround the house of a man who is beating his wife,
calling out publicly to shame him. In cases of severe
abuse, they help the woman to escape by providing her
sanctuary in neighborhood homes until the conflict is
resolved or she can permanently relocate (Kerns 1992).
In Mira de las Flores, a shantytown in Lima, Peru,
women have organized themselves into a neighborhood
watch committee, and they wear whistles to summon other
women if attacked (Heise 1989). Levinson, in his cross-
cultural study cited earlier, observes that "the presence
of kin or neighbors who will intervene in violent or
potentially violent situations is a characteristic of societies
with low rates of wife beating" (1988, p. 452).

In Canada aboriginal communities are addressing
domestic violence by drawing on traditional models of
conflict resolution. In Manitoba women from the Hollow
Water Reserve have begun to use the tribe's "circle of
healing" to address domestic violence. The community
members confront the abuser, requiring him to
acknowledge his crime publicly, and offer their support
for healing both the victim and the perpetrator. The abuser
is given a "healing contract" setting out the punishment—
usually community work—and arrangements are made
to protect the victim. When the contract expires, a
cleansing ceremony takes place to symbolize the return
of balance to the abuser, the family, and the community.
At this point healing is considered complete and the crime
is to be forgotten. Healing can take years (MATCH
International 1990).

Treatment programs for perpetrators

There has been increasing interest in recent years in
rehabilitating offenders through treatment and reeducation.
Treatment programs have proliferated in industrial countries
as courts have sought a social solution to wife abuse that
does not lead to further crowding of jails. Many women,
too, have favored their partner getting help—rather than
punishment—as a first step. In the United States most court-
mandated programs meet weekly for 12 weeks; others
range from as few as six sessions to more than eight months
(Heise and Chapman 1992). A few treatment programs
patterned after the U.S. and Canadian models have sprung
up in developing countries as well (for example, in Mexico).

Most treatment programs are based on the idea that
violent behavior is a learned and socially reinforced behavior.
Counseling styles vary from structured classes that educate
men on the power dynamics of battering to free-flowing
self-help groups run by experienced facilitators. Some
groups concentrate on improving men's ability to handle
emotions; others go further, challenging men's perceived
right to control women through violence. Many programs
include training in relaxation, education on male socialization,
and such behavioral techniques as "time outs" to interrupt
escalation of anger (Stordeur and Stille 1989).

Only recently have researchers attempted to evaluate
the effectiveness of programs to treat batterers. Treatment
appears to reduce the physical violence of some men, but
other variables, such as interaction with the justice system,
probably also play a role (Harrel 1991). A recent review
by Tolman and Bennett (1990) reports that 53 to 85 percent
of men who complete treatment are not violent six to 18
months later, with lower rates for longer follow-up periods
and for studies based on victim reports of violence.[22] But
these same studies show that even "nonviolent" men continue
to use verbal threats and psychological abuse to control
their wives. As Edleson and Grusznski speculate, "many
men who end their violence may resort to the use of threats
as a 'legal' but hardly less terrorizing form of control"
(1988, p. 20). Moreover, the success rates in such studies
apply only to those who complete the programs. Because
more than half of the men participating in such programs
drop out before completing their treatment, it remains unclear
how successful programs are across a wide range of men
(Saunders and Azar 1989).

Perhaps the most definitive evaluation to date found
that court-ordered treatment had no positive effect on rates
of physical violence or threats of violence (as measured
by self-reports, victim reports, and police records), or
on key beliefs about wife beating and personal control
of violence (Harrel 1991). Unlike other studies, this study
compared men ordered by the court to obtain treatment
with a group of men not ordered to attend treatment—a
true control group. In addition, it compared men's rate

of violence before court intervention with their rate of violence after court involvement but before treatment, thus allowing researchers to evaluate whether the effects measured were due solely to treatment or due in part to the justice system's involvement. The study found that rates of violence were lower after arrest and court hearing, but that treatment itself added no additional benefit. These findings suggest that most of the positive benefits attributed to treatment may actually come from the justice system's intervention rather than from treatment.

It would be premature, however, to conclude that treatment holds no promise for reducing future domestic violence. Treatment and evaluation methods are still in their infancy, and new treatment approaches may yet prove effective. And investigators note that failure to impose harsh penalties for abuse or for failure to attend treatment may undermine the efficacy of treatment. Harrel's (1991) results indicated that none of the men in the treatment or the nontreatment groups believed that they would suffer significant legal or social consequences from committing violence in the future.

In addition to batterer treatment, there is a long tradition in North America and Europe of attempting to treat sex offenders. Techniques have ranged from psychosurgery and pharmacologic interventions (for example, treatment with medrosyprogesterone acetate, or MPA, an androgen antagonist) to cognitive and behavioral therapy. In the United States roughly three-quarters of all sex offender treatment programs are community-based, although 40 states were treating adult sex offenders in prison in 1990 (down from 48 in the mid-1980s; Sapp and Vaughn 1991). In recent years increasing emphasis has been placed on identifying and treating adolescent sex offenders to stop aggressive sexual behavior before it escalates. Research on 411 adult sex offenders treated as outpatients shows that 58 percent began their deviant sexual behavior during early adolescence and that the average adolescent male sex offender has 380 victims during his lifetime (Abel and others 1985, as cited in Stops and Mays 1991). Definitive evaluations of the outcomes of treatment for adult offenders, although scarce, show that at least some programs appear to reduce recidivism (based on rearrest rates) among pedophiles and exhibitionists, but none has proved effective with hard-core rapists (Marshall and others 1990).

Treatment programs and evaluation methods for sex offenders—like those for batterers—are still in their infancy, so the possibility that they can provide effective intervention should not be dismissed. Nonetheless, addressing perpetrators one by one after their patterns of abusive behavior have been forged (and reinforced by social norms) is not a particularly promising approach to addressing violence against women. Although treatment may help prevent the future abuse of one or more women, true prevention requires creating a generation of individuals who see violent behavior as inappropriate.

7. Research needs

This review has revealed that, although existing data are sufficient to capture the severity of violence against women around the world, more and better research is needed to spur political action in specific countries, to refine our understanding of the consequences of gender violence, and to evaluate the effectiveness of different interventions (see box 9 for the most important data needs). Well-designed studies of the prevalence of wife abuse are beginning to emerge, but there is still a large need in the developing countries for population-based data on the prevalence of sexual assault and child sexual abuse, and for studies of the mental and physical health consequences of gender-based violence. In addition, we need to begin collecting qualitative data on how women

experience violence: How does physical abuse affect women's productivity? What strategies do women use to cope with abuse? How do different women define violence?

As a first step toward meeting these needs, institutions such as the World Bank could create forums for researchers to come together with practitioners and advocates—at both the national and the international level—to develop a joint research agenda and discuss outstanding methodological issues. Creating a dialogue up front between those familiar with the issues (shelter workers, advocates) and those who understand research will help ensure that future research is both relevant and defensible. Too often, research pursued by academics

---

Box 9 Priority research needs on gender-based violence and health

- Better data on the incidence and prevalence of gender-related violence in representative populations of women.
- Data on the percentage of women presenting in different settings (emergency rooms, family planning clinics) who have been raped or abused, or both. (Such data should help convince health care providers of the prevalence of abuse as well as help assess the potential of different settings as points of identification and referral for victims.)
- Data on the health care and social costs of domestic violence and sexual assault and abuse, including estimates of the cost of emergency services, indirect costs of productivity losses, and costs associated with increased utilization of primary care services.
- Descriptive profiles of the typical symptoms of rape and abuse victims (location of injuries, somatic complaints) to facilitate identification of victims by health care providers.

- Data on the mental health consequences of violence, especially in a developing world context, including relative risk among victimized and nonvictimized women for anxiety, depression, suicide attempts, sexual dysfunction, somatic health complaints, and alcohol and drug abuse.
- Data on the impact of domestic violence and sexual assault on birth outcomes, pregnancy complications, and rates of miscarriage and low birth weight.
- Studies that analyze the relation between gender violence and such development issues as safe motherhood, child survival, AIDS prevention, and family planning.
- Studies that evaluate the effectiveness of different interventions, including self-help support groups, violence prevention curricula, and screening for abuse at primary care facilities.

asks the wrong questions and research pursued by practitioners lacks rigor. Future progress in research on violence would benefit greatly from:

- Better-articulated definitions of rape, child sexual abuse, and other forms of gender violence to facilitate measurement and comparisons across populations
- Greater consensus on operational definitions of different forms of violence for the purposes of research
- More research on which methodologies elicit the most disclosure on violence-related topics
- Increased collaboration between researchers and women's NGOs, service providers, and victims of violence
- Greater emphasis on evaluating the effects of different interventions.

There are also many unexploited opportunities for integrating questions related to violence into research funded for other purposes, such as focus groups and surveys designed to inform AIDS prevention work, or surveys conducted for family planning or health purposes. An improved Demographic and Health Survey module on violence and application of the instrument in a large number of countries, for example, could generate invaluable information. In addition, multicountry studies are urgently needed to explore how women and men interpret violence, its causes and correlates, and the attitudinal and legal barriers victims face when interacting with public institutions.

8. Conclusions

By taking violence against women seriously, the World Bank can help encourage governments, other lenders, and the world community to do likewise. As a financial and policymaking institution with considerable leverage, the Bank could lend visibility and legitimacy to the issue by incorporating violence into its policy-oriented sector work on poverty, health, education, and women in development, and by supporting projects addressing violence against women. Already the Bank is supporting the construction of a government-run shelter for battered women in Papua New Guinea. The Bank can also urge governments to take action in all of the ways suggested here, in consultation with women's NGOs and advisors with experience in combating violence, pushing legal reform, and working with victims.

Much of the necessary preventive action will require persistent and extensive work through the Bank's sectoral divisions, and a commitment to community-based organizations, public education, and women's empowerment. In the short run some of the most effective action can be taken by health and family planning agencies and providers. As Racquel Edralin Tiglao, director of the Women's Crisis Center in Metro Manila, observes, recognizing violence as a health issue is an essential first step. When asked by an interviewer about the most important thing that we can do about violence against women, she replied that:

> People should start taking violence seriously, particularly health organizations because it is a life-threatening issue. When you're talking of family planning, why are there women who cannot do family planning? You must see whether some of these women are actually battered women who have no choices. Or those who seek abortions? They could be rape or incest victims. They should be asked. If health workers would be more vigilant in detecting incidents of violence against women, we could make people more aware that this is a very crucial issue for women's health and women's lives. (Datinguinoo 1991, p. 6)

Appendix A Recommendations for government action to combat violence against women

Actions for the national secretariat on women

1. In consultation with women's NGOS working on gender violence issues, develop a national initiative against violence against women. (Countries that do not have a high-level office dedicated to advancing the status of women should consider establishing one.)

2. Provide financial and technical support to NGOs that provide services to and perform advocacy on behalf of victims of violence, especially those working from a feminist perspective. Work with women's NGOs to develop strategies to expand the availability of services for victims—from both governmental and nongovernmental sources—including shelters, crisis centers, legal assistance, counseling, and support groups.

3. Work with other ministries to implement a co-ordinated campaign against violence against women, including all of the activities outlined below.

4. Work to improve women's access to productive resources, including land, credit, wage employment, and child care.

5. Sponsor a national media campaign designed to communicate social norms that define violence against women as unacceptable.

Actions for the ministry of health

1. Establish and implement model protocols for the early identification and referral of abuse victims in health care settings, including emergency rooms and primary care facilities such as family planning and prenatal clinics. Train staff in counseling, examining victims, and collecting legal evidence for prosecution.

2. Undertake research on the incidence and prevalence of gender-related violence, the percentage of women presenting in different health settings who are abused, the mental health consequences of violence, and the health care costs of domestic violence and rape.

3. Integrate questions on gender violence into national health surveys and into ongoing research in such areas as AIDS, sexuality, and family planning. Colombia incorporated questions on family violence into its Demographic and Health Survey, and the Philippines is planning to do likewise. The module needs to be improved and its use funded.

4. Introduce consciousness-raising material and training on the dynamics of abuse (including culture-bound practices that are harmful) into the curricula and professional licensing exams for such health care workers as doctors, psychologists, nurses, and midwives. Integrate similar themes into the training of community-based health promoters.

5. Establish, through research, a clinical profile—detailing injuries, location, and other symptoms—of women presenting with abuse to help health workers identify victims.

6. Incorporate themes related to all forms of gender-based violence and sex role stereotyping into radio shows, soap operas, and other educational materials now being used to promote family planning, AIDS education, and other health themes.

7. In collaboration with the ministry of justice, sponsor sensitivity training for forensic doctors on violence against women and on how to collect and document evidence of assault, sexual abuse, and rape.

8. Discourage destructive drinking and illicit drug use among adolescents and adults by sponsoring educational programs and skills training on resisting peer pressure.

9. Expand treatment programs for individuals addicted to drugs and alcohol.

10. Implement treatment and reeducation programs for perpetrators.

Actions for the ministry of justice

1. Sponsor legislation that specifically criminalizes domestic violence, marital rape, and other crimes against women. Eliminate inappropriate legal responses, such as the "honor defense," which exculpates perpetrators of wife murder and infanticide.

2. Reform existing laws to facilitate prosecution of gender-based crimes such as rape and domestic assault. Amend laws that interfere with the ability of women to escape violent relationships (for example, barriers to divorce).

3. Document how laws related to gender violence are (or are not) enforced, detailing the frequency of prosecution, arrest rates, judgments, and sentences.

4. Amend laws and regulations, as needed, to allow any licensed health care provider to examine and collect evidence of physical and sexual assault for legal purposes.

5. Extend and improve medical and legal services provided by the state for victims of violence in both urban and rural areas.

6. Require all crime statistics to be broken down by gender (for both the perpetrator and the victim). Information should also be recorded on the relationship between the perpetrator and the victim to help identify the gendered nature of violent crime.

7. Support NGOs providing human rights education and legal literacy training for women.

8. Implement training programs on gender-based violence for the police, prosecutors, and judges.

9. Incorporate gender-awareness training and analysis into law school curriculum.

10. Take measures to increase the number of women police officers, lawyers, prosecutors, and judges. Ensure the availability of female officers and forensic doctors for gender-violence-related investigations and exams.

Actions for the ministry of education

1. Remove gender bias and gender stereotyping from school curriculum and teaching materials.

2. Integrate gender awareness training, parenting skills, and nonviolent conflict resolution into school curricula.

3. Work with the media to portray positive images of equitable relationships and to remove gratuitous violence from the media.

4. Provide gender-awareness training to teachers and educators and teach them to recognize the signs of abuse.

Appendix B Definition of violence against women

Despite the existence of a worldwide movement against gender-based violence, there is no single definition of violence that guides all activists. The main point of contention is how broadly to define the term. Some argue for a very broad definition that includes any act or omission that causes harm to women or keeps them in a subordinate position (see, for example, the definition in the draft Pan American Treaty against Violence). Under such a definition, any structural feature that perpetuates gender-based discrimination could arguably qualify as violence.

The appeal of a broad definition is that it would permit many violations of women's human rights to be addressed under the rubric of violence. But the danger is that in throwing the net so widely, the descriptive power of the term is lost. Calling everything violence—poverty, pornography, trafficking in women, lack of access to schooling—makes it easier to discount the issue entirely and to justify inaction on the more specific forms of abuse, such as rape and wife assault. (It is rather like the justification that since everything causes cancer anyway, one might as well smoke.) This is not to say that unequal pay and lack of access to safe abortion, for example, are not violations of women's human rights, but we must ask what explanatory power is gained by calling these violations violence.

An overly broad definition limits the usefulness of the term for describing such traditional forms of violence as rape and wife assault. We have a word to describe gender inequalities—discrimination. And we have a word that captures much of what activists call structural violence—poverty. But no other term collectively defines those acts of force or coercion, perpetrated by individual men, that cause physical and emotional harm to women. Thus, I would argue for a more limited definition, recognizing full well that violence is just one of many violations of women's human rights.

The United Nations Declaration against Violence against Women avoids making difficult distinctions by offering a tautology in place of a definition. According to the declaration, violence against women is "any act of gender-based violence that results in, or is likely to result in, physical, sexual or psychological harm or suffering to women, including threats of such acts, coercion or arbitrary deprivations of liberty, whether occurring in public or private life." It then offers a list of abuses that presumably meet the definition (appendix box B.1). But the list is not exhaustive, and it leaves unanswered the fundamental question of what constitutes gender-based violence.

The United Nations list of abuses does represent an adequate compromise between a desire to be inclusive and the need to keep the definition specific, however. It includes only acts perpetrated by an individual or the state and excludes laws, policies, or structural inequalities that could be construed as violent (laws against abortion, structural adjustment policies). But the UN definition provides insufficient guidance to determine whether items that are not listed, such as female feticide or restrictive abortion policies, would constitute gender violence.

What would constitute an adequate definition of violence? Any definition must have at its center the core concepts of force and coercion, which distinguish between violent and merely oppressive behavior. But to what extent should violence be limited to physical force? Dictionary and public health definitions of violence tend to focus exclusively on physical force. *Webster's Ninth Collegiate Dictionary*, for example, defines violence as "the exertion of physical force so as to cause injury or abuse." Concentrating on physical force provides a clear demarcation between violence and other acts, but it excludes many behaviors—such as psychological abuse and humiliation—that activists and women generally include in their definitions of violence. Indeed, studies have shown that battered women often rate emotional abuse by their partners as more injurious than physical assault (Casey 1988). To exclude verbal and psychological abuse would be to deny an important facet of women's victimization.

It remains, however, to distinguish between random violence and violence that is gender-based. Clearly, the notion of violence against women does not include violence directed toward men or directed toward women for reasons unrelated to their sex (for example, an assault during a robbery). What distinguishes violence against women is force or coercion (whether verbal or physical) that is socially tolerated in part *because the victims are female.* At times this force may be consciously applied to perpetuate male power and control; at other times that intent may be missing, but the effect nonetheless is to cause harm in a way that reinforces female subordination.

The case of genital mutilation underscores the importance of arguing for a definition of violence that rests on the notion of physical and psychological harm rather than on the express intent of the perpetrator. Although most parents do not subject their daughters to female circumcision with a conscious desire to harm, the effect of the practice—intended or not—is to physically, psychologically, and sexually maim young girls. Moreover, parents proceed with the operation knowing full well that it will cause pain and suffering, even though this may not be their primary motivation (see the definition offered in Asia Pacific Forum on Women, Law and Development 1990, which hinges specifically on the intent of the perpetrator).

In keeping with the above discussion, I propose to define violence against women as:

> Any act of verbal or physical force, coercion, or life-threatening deprivation, directed at an individual woman or girl, that causes physical or psychological harm, humiliation or arbitrary deprivation of liberty and that perpetuates female subordination.

This definition has a number of important advantages. By referring to acts directed at an individual girl or woman, it helps distinguish between acts of violence and harmful policies that may damage the health of women as a class but are not directed at a particular individual (for example, lack of investment in women's health research). By including life-threatening deprivation along with force or coercion, the definition includes systematic neglect of girl children in cultures that value sons over daughters. This type of deprivation (including withholding of food and medical care) leads directly to death and starvation on a significant scale, and it is perpetrated against individual girls, distinguishing it from other acts of omission that more properly constitute discrimination or structural inequality (for example, lack of access to schooling). Finally, the clause "and perpetuates female subordination" speaks to the social consequences of the violence and helps distinguish random violence from gender-based violence.

The definition includes the phrase "arbitrary deprivation of liberty" to accommodate such acts as forced isolation or excessively controlling behavior by a batterer

—acts that fail to respect women as autonomous, adult human beings. Some men use violence or threats of violence to exert almost total control over their wives' mobility and their access to money and other material resources. Such behavior can reach excessive and dangerous proportions.

Appendix box B.1 Definitions of violence against women

Behavior by the man, adopted to control his victim, which results in physical, sexual and/or psychological damage, forced isolation, or economic deprivation or behavior which leaves a woman living in fear. (Australia 1991)

Any act involving use of force or coercion with an intent of perpetuating/promoting hierarchical gender relations. (Asia Pacific Forum on Women, Law and Development 1990)

Any act of gender-based violence that results in, or is likely to result in, physical, sexual or psychological harm or suffering to women, including threats of such acts, coercion or arbitrary deprivations of liberty, whether occurring in public or private life. Violence against women shall be understood to encompass but not be limited to:

Physical, sexual and psychological violence occurring in the family and in the community, including battering, sexual abuse of female children, dowry-related violence, marital rape, female genital mutilation and other traditional practices harmful to women, non-spousal violence, violence related to exploitation, sexual harassment and intimidation at work, in educational institutions and elsewhere, trafficking in women, forced prostitution, and violence perpetrated or condoned by the State. (UN Declaration against Violence against Women)

Any act, omission or conduct by means of which physical sexual or mental suffering is inflicted, directly or indirectly, through deceit, seduction, threat, coercion or any other means, on any woman with the purpose or effect of intimidating, punishing or humiliating her or of maintaining her in sex-stereotyped roles or of denying her human dignity, sexual self-determination, physical, mental and moral integrity or of undermining the security of her person, her self-respect or her personality, or of diminishing her physical or mental capacities. (Draft Pan American Treaty against Violence against Women)

Any act or omission which prejudices the life, the physical or psychological integrity or the liberty of a person or which seriously harms the development of his or her personality. (Council of Europe 1986)

Appendix C Methodology for estimating the healthy years of life lost due to domestic violence and rape

The calculation of the disability-adjusted life years (DALYs) lost due to domestic violence and rape is based on estimates of the share of life years lost to premature mortality and morbidity that can be attributed directly to gender-based victimization. The burden of disease is the net present value of the future stream of disability caused by incident cases in 1990 plus the future stream of healthy life lost from premature mortality from 1990 deaths by disease condition. A 3 percent per year discount rate is assumed in the exercise to translate future years of life lost into their present value. Nonuniform age weights are also assumed, but because the loss of life is valued according to the future stream of age-specific weights and not just the weight of one year, the results of the analysis are not very sensitive to the introduction of nonuniform age weights. To equate morbidity and mortality, the global burden of disease (GBD) exercise assigns "disability weighting factors" (between 0.02 and 0.9) to conditions based on their interference with normal enjoyment of life and functioning. A rating of 0.02 represents minimal interference with well-being and productivity, and weightings of 0.6 and higher represent major life dislocations, with 0.9 appropriate only for conditions just short of death, such as coma.

A full discussion of the methodology, including the estimation of incidence by region and by age group and assumptions about disability weights, age-weighting, and the discount rate, is contained in Murray forthcoming and Murray and Lopez forthcoming.

Since domestic violence and rape are not diseases per se, the GDB frames gender-based victimization as a risk factor that increases the incidence of certain other morbidities and conditions, such as physical traumas and depression. Thus, the calculation of DALYs lost to gender-based victimization begins with the GDB estimates of DALYs lost due to each condition and then estimates the percentage of the total for that condition attributable to domestic violence or rape. (An analogy would be estimating the proportion of disability resulting from emphysema, lung cancer, and heart disease that can be attributed to smoking.)

Appendix table C.1 summarizes the estimates of attributable risk used to calculate the DALYs lost due to rape and domestic violence. The evidence supporting each percentage estimate is on file with the World Bank GBD team. The DALYs lost to each condition is multiplied by the percentage attributable to gender victimization and then summed across conditions. The total DALYs lost to domestic violence and rape can then be compared to totals calculated for different disease categories, such as tuberculosis and malaria.

The table gives estimates only for DALYs lost due to rape and domestic violence among women age 15 to 44. Thus it excludes DALYs lost due to other gender-based forms of victimization, such as genital mutilation.

Appendix table C.1 Disability-adjusted life years lost to women age 15 to 44 due to conditions attributable to domestic violence and rape

Relevant conditions	Total DALYs lost to women age 15 to 44 (millions)	Share attributable to domestic violence and rape
STDs (excluding HIV)	15.8	2 percent
HIV	10.6	2 percent
Abortion	2.5	10 percent
Depression (men age 15 to 44)	10.7 5.4	50 percent of difference between women and men
Alcohol dependence	0.9	10 percent
Drug dependence	1.1	10 percent
Post-traumatic stress disorder	2.1	60 percent
Unintentional injuries	6.7	20 percent of total burden minus burden attributable to motor vehicle accidents and occupational injuries
Suicide	5.5	30 percent
Homicide	0.9	60 percent
Intentional injury	1.2	90 percent
Total	58.0	6 percent

Source: World Bank data.

Appendix D Sample danger assessment

[This sample danger assessment is from Campbell 1986.]

Several risk factors have been associated with homicides (murder) of both batterers and battered women as a result of research that was conducted after the killings took place. We cannot predict what will happen in your case, but we would like you to be aware of the danger of homicide in situations of severe battering and for you to see how many of the risk factors apply to your situation. (The "he" in the questions refers to your husband, partner, ex-husband, ex-partner, or whoever is physically hurting you.) Please circle the relevant answer below.

1. Has the physical violence increased in frequency over the past year?   YES   NO

2. Has the physical violence increased in severity over the past year and/or has a weapon or threat with a weapon been used?   YES   NO

3. Does he ever try to choke you?   YES   NO

4. Is there a gun in the house?   YES   NO

5. Has he ever forced you into sex when you did not wish to do so?   YES   NO

6. Does he use drugs (cocaine, crack heroin, uppers or other street drugs)?   YES   NO

7. Does he threaten to kill you and/or do you believe he is capable of killing you?   YES   NO

8. Is he drunk every day or almost every day (in terms of quantity of alcohol?)   YES   NO

9. Does he control most of your daily activities? For instance, does he tell you who you can be friends with, how much money you can take shopping or when you can have the car?   YES   NO

10. Have you ever been beaten by him while you were pregnant?   YES   NO

    (If never pregnant by him, check here._____)

11. Is he violently and consistently jealous of you? For instance does he say, "If I can't have you, no one can?"   YES   NO

12. Have you ever threatened or tried suicide?   YES   NO

13. Has he ever threatened or tried suicide?   YES   NO

14. Is he violent toward your children?   YES   NO

15. Is he violent outside the home?   YES   NO

Total "YES" answers _____

Appendix E Treatment protocols for battered women

This article is reprinted with the permission of *Response*.

NURSING NETWORK ON VIOLENCE AGAINST WOMEN

Treatment Protocols For Battered Women

WENDY K. TAYLOR AND JACQUELYN C. CAMPBELL

Battering of an intimate partner is a widespread social problem occurring on a daily basis (Varvaro, 1989). Society has a tendency to look upon spouse abuse as a "private matter" or "love spat" that will soon be over. This is not the case. It is rare for a violent episode between intimates to happen only once (Varvaro, 1989). Over time the violence escalates, becomes more frequent, and severity of injury increases (Varvaro, 1989; Stark, Flitcraft & Frazier,1979).

Research conducted by McLeer and Anwar (1989); Stark, Flitcraft, and Frazier (1979); and Goldberg, and Tomlanovich (1984) indicate that 25 percent–33 percent of female trauma injuries were the result of battering. Stark and Flitcraft (1985) have found that domestic violence accounts for more injuries to women than rapes, muggings and motor vehicle accidents combined. In general, it is believed that the severity of injury is greater in domestic violence cases than injuries sustained in stranger assault (Varvaro, 1989).

In 1980 the National Crime Survey (NCS) reported that 30,000 visits to emergency rooms, 40,000 physician visits, 21,000 hospitalizations, and 100,000 days of hospitalization were associated with domestic violence (McLeer and Anwar, 1989; Varvaro, 1989). More than one million women per year seek medical care for injuries caused by battering (Deckstein and Nadelson, 1986). Traumatic injuries from family violence range from mild to life-threatening. Injuries include, but are not limited to, bruises in various stages of healing, fractures, black eyes, ear injuries, abdominal injuries, miscarriages related to trauma to the abdominal area, stab wounds, gunshot wounds, head trauma, and suicide attempts (Campbell and Sheridan, 1989; Varvaro, 1989; and Helton, McFarlane, and Anderson, 1987).

Many battered women do not need or seek medical attention for their injuries. Of those seeking medical care only one in ten is officially identified as a battered woman by health care professionals (Randall, 1990; Varvaro, 1989; Stark, Flitcraft, & Frazier, 1979). Once identified, the treatment of battered women by health care personnel may be a positive response, a negative response, or non-existent (Varvaro, 1989). Kurz and Stark (1988) have found evidence of inappropriate responses to battered women by the medical profession. Their findings indicate that in most cases the battering is denied or its importance is diminished. They also found that battering was not a high priority for health care providers. Medical responses to battered women tend to focus on the physical injuries caused by battering and have a tendency to blame the victim for the violence (Kurz & Stark, 1988; Varvaro, 1989; Campbell and Sheridan, 1989; Rosewater, 1988). Reasons for inappropriate responses or no response by the health care professional may stem from lack of knowledge or training in abuse issues, misinformation/myths, sexist bias, the structure of the medical model (Campbell and Sheridan, 1989; Kurz, & Stark, 1988), and disbelieving the woman's story (Hilberman, 1980). Research has indicated that a positive response from the health care provider may enable the battered woman to take steps in ending a violent relationship and choosing a non-violent alternative lifestyle for her children and herself (Campbell and Sheridan, 1989; Varvaro, 1989).

Nurses, physicians, and other health care providers are in an ideal setting to intervene with battered women. Unidentified battered women have increased health problems and make more frequent visits to health care facilities (Campbell and Sheridan, 1989; and Varvaro, 1989). All females, regardless of presentation, should be assessed for battering. The majority of battered women will discuss the violence in their relationships if asked. It is important to treat not only the battered woman's physical injuries but attend to her emotional needs as well. Always interview the woman alone and reassure her that she is safe in disclosing this information to you. Most battered women will feel a sense of relief that someone believes them and is willing to offer assistance. It is of utmost importance to document the history of the current abusive incident and past abuses in her medical record. State in her medical record who injured her. All battered women should recieve a complete physical exam, including a neurological exam, and x-rays to identify old and new fractures. Be sure to assess for possible sexual abuse by her partner. Document all physical findings. If at all possible, photograph the woman's injuries. You will need to obtain signed consent to photograph. If unable to photograph, use a body map to indicate location of current injuries and past injuries. If the battered woman has children, assess for child abuse. The battered woman needs to be informed of her rights according to state laws, and she should be given referral information for counseling and shelters (Campbell and Sheridan, 1989; and Varvaro, 1989).

The development and use of a written policy and protocols increased the identification of battered women more than five-fold in one urban emergency department (McLeer & Anwar, 1989). In another emergency department of a large, urban, university hospital, Tilden and

Shepherd (1987) tested an interview protocol used by emergency room staff nurses when assessing female trauma patients. The researchers wanted to determine if using a systematic protocol that directly questioned women as to who caused their injury, would lead to an increase in the identification of battered women. Data were collected from the medical records of all female trauma patients for a 4-month period prior to implementing protocols in order to establish a baseline. After training the nurses in the use of the protocol, data were again collected for a 4-month period. The total N for the pre- and post- training was 72 and 74 respectively. Post-training rate of identification was significantly higher (22.9 percent) than the pre-training rate of 9.72 percent (Tilden & Shepherd, 1987).

McLeer and Anwar (1987) reviewed the records of every fourth female trauma case during 1976 who presented to the emergency room of the Medical College of Pennsylvania. A total of 359 medical records were reviewed. The results indicated that 5.6 percent were classified as positive for battering, 10.9 percent were probable battered women, and 9.2 percent suggestive of battering. A protocol containing questions eliciting a trauma history and whether someone was responsible for causing a woman's injuries was developed. The emergency room nurses were trained to use this protocol. After training and implementation of this protocol, 412 emergency room records were examined. The authors report that positive identification for battering increased from 5.6 percent to 30 percent after implementation of staff training and use of protocols (McLeer, & Anwar, 1987).

In 1986 McLeer & Anwar conducted a follow-up study at the same emergency room. They found the identifica-tion rate of battered women was significantly lower in 1985 than in 1977. The protocol implemented in 1977 was no longer in effect. Since the patient population had not changed, the authors concluded that without a monitoring system to ensure continued use, implementation of a written policy and protocols were not sufficient for continued vigilance on the part of staff in identifying battered women (McLeer & Anwar, 1989).

Goldberg and Tomlanovich (1984) conducted a study using 492 male and female emergency room patients. The purpose of their study was to obtain information on the extent and nature of domestic violence in the emergency room patient population. Data were collected through chart audit and a self-administered questionnaire. The results indicated that 22 percent of the patients identified themselves as victims of domestic violence on the questionnaire but only 5 percent were identified as such in their emergency room records. The data from these studies indicate that development of protocols, the implementation of protocols, and education of staff in using the protocols increases the rate of identification of battered women.

The Joint commission for the Accreditation of Health Care Organizations (JCAHO) has mandated that hospitals develop and implement policies and procedures for the identification, assessment, treatment, evaluation, and referral of battered women and the abused/neglected elderly. The mandate became effective January 1, 1992. A copy of the new JCAHO emergency department criteria has been included to assist you in the development and writing of protocols specific to your state and institution (Tables 1 and 2).

Following is a brief synopsis of protocols and training

TABLE 1
Accreditation Manual for Hospitals, 1992 Emergency Services

ES.5.1.2.10 the handling of adult and child victims of alleged or suspected abuse or neglect.
  ES.5.1.2.10.1 Criteria are developed for identifying possible victims of abuse.
    ES.5.1.2.10.1.1 The criteria address at least the following types of abuse:
      ES.5.1.2.10.1.1.1 physical assault;
      ES.5.1.2.10.1.1.2 rape or other sexual molestation; and
      ES.5.1.2.10.1.1.3 domestic abuse of elders, spouses, partners and children.
  ES.5.1.2.10.2 Procedures for the evaluation of patients who meet the criteria address:
  ES.5.1.2.10.2.1 patient consent;
  ES.5.1.2.10.2.2 examination and treatment;
  ES.5.1.2.10.2.3 the hospital's responsibility for the collection, retention, and safeguarding of specimens, photographs, and other evidentiary material released by the patient; and
  ES.5.1.2.10.2.4 as legally required, notification of, and release of information to, the proper authorities.
  ES.5.1.2.10.3 A list is maintained in the emergency department/service of private and public community agencies that provide, or arrange for, evaluation and care for victims of, abuse, and referrals are made as appropriate.
  ES.5.1.2.10.4 The medical record includes documentation of examinations, treatment given, any referrals made to other care providers and to community agencies, and any required reporting to the proper authorities.
  ES.5.1.2.10.5 There is a plan for education of appropriate staff about the criteria for identifying, and the procedures for handling, possible victims of abuse.

TABLE 2
Accreditation manual for Hospitals, 1992 Hospital-Sponsored Ambulatory Care Services

HO.3.2.15 The handling of adult and child victims of alleged or suspected abuse or neglect.
  HO.3.2.15.1 Criteria are developed for identifying possible victims of abuse:
    HO.3.2.15.1.1 The criteria address at least the following types of abuse:
      HO.3.2.15.1.1.1 physical assault;
      HO.3.2.15.1.1.2 rape or other sexual molestation; and
      HO.3.2.15.1.1.3 domestic abuse of elders, spouses, partners, and children.
  HO.3.2.15.2 Procedures for the evaluation of patients who meet the criteria address:
    HO.3.2.15.2.1 patient consent;
    HO.3.2.15.2.2 examination and treatment;
    HO.3.2.15.2.3 the hospital's responsibility for the collection, retention, and safeguarding of specimens, photographs, and other evidentiary material released by the patient; and
    HO.3.2.15.2.4 as legally required, notification of, and release of, information to the proper authorities.
  HO.3.2.15.3. A list is maintained in the abulatory care services department of private and public community agencies that provide, or arrange for, evaluation and care for victims of abuse, and referrals are made as appropriate.
  HO.3.2.15.4 The medical record includes documentation of examination, treatment given, any referral(s) made to other care providers and to community agencies, and any required reporting to the proper authorities.
  HO.3.2.15.5 There is a plan for education of appropriate staff about the criteria for identifying and the procedures for handling possible victims of abuse.

manuals from various institutions nationwide used for the treatment of battered women in health care settings: Sivan, A. B. (Ed). (1990). *Child Abuse, Sexual Assault & Domestic Violence: Guidelines for Treatment in Emergency and Primary Medical Settings*. Order from: Metropolitan Chicago Healthcare Council, 222 S. Riverside Plaza, Chicago, IL 60606, (312) 906-6000. (Cost of this manual is $75.00 for members of the Metropolitan Chicago Healthcare Council; $95.00 for tax-exempt non-members; and $102.60 for all others. There is also a $5.00 postage and handling charge on all orders.)

This manual is a joint publication of the Metropolitan Chicago Healthcare Council, the Chicago Metropolitan Battered Women's Network, and Chicago Sexual Assault Services Network. It updates and replaces, *Guidelines for the treatment of battered women victims in emergency room settings*, authored by Sheridan, Belknap, Engel, Katz, and Kelleher (1985). The revised edition comes in a three-ring binder. It was primarily written for use by emergency room personnel, but is applicable and adaptable to any clinical setting. It is comprehensive in its scope as it includes treatment guidelines for child abuse and neglect; child sexual assault; battered women; elder abuse; adult sexual assault; and a discussion entitled, *Staff reactions to problems of domestic violence and child abuse*.

The manual is divided into four sections. Each section begins with facts; followed by types of common and subtle injuries indicative of abuse; assessment, treatment and management issues; documentation; and prevention strategies. The four sections include Illinois statutes and acts related to the type of abuse, sample protocols, injury maps, selected references, and a list of referrals to community agencies which provide services to battered women, their children, and sexual assault survivors.

Colorado Department of Health, and Colorado Domestic Violence Coalition. (1991). *Domestic violence: A guide for health care providers*, (3rd Ed). For ordering information contact: Colorado Domestic Violence Coalition, P.O. Box 18902, Denver, CO 80218. (303) 573-9018.

This is a comprehensive guide for health care providers that can be adapted to any health care setting. The manual comes in a three-ring binder and is divided into seven sections, including an appendix. It is a practical, as well as informative, "how to" guide.

Section I provides an introduction, an overview of the problem, and facts/objectives. Section II discusses the legal responsibilities of health care personnel. Section III covers the context, characteristics, dynamics, costs, and effects of battering. Identification, assessment, documentation, and intervention are addressed in Section IV. Section V provides specific guidelines for developing, implementing and maintaining a protocol. An extensive bibliography is listed in Section VI. In Section VII the reader will find a list of resources, contacts, and training films. Several articles related to battering are included in the appendix. The resources and statutes referred to in this manual are specific to Colorado.

King, C., and Ryan, J. (1991). *Woman abuse advocacy protocol*. Order from: Christine King, Ed.D, RN, School of Nursing, University of Massachusetts, Arnold House, Amherst, MA 01003, (413) 545-2703.

The advocacy protocol is a brief, yet precise guide for nurses and social workers intervening with battered women. Included are communication techniques for interviewing the abused woman; type of information to be documented in the medical record; specific services available to battered women; a section on legal rights and options; various types of counseling alternatives; assessment for risk of homicide and discussing safety strategies/plan; ways to help the battered woman establish a support network; and methods to empower the woman when closing. This protocol will be appearing in an up-coming issue of the American Journal of Nursing.

Also written by King, Ryan, and Perri, (1987), is a training manual for nurses entitled, *Reaching Out To Battered Women*, Stone Circle Press. The manual includes information on assessment, intervention, documentation, and referral. For a copy, refer to the above address.

Foley, Hoag, and Eliot. (1991). *Empowering battered women: suggestions for health care providers.* Order from: Massachusetts Coalition of Battered Women Service Groups, 107 South Street, 5th Floor, Boston, MA 02111, (617) 426-8492. (Cost is $12.00 per copy plus $2.90 for postage and handling.)

An educational manual written by attorneys in the Foley, Hoag, and Eliot Abuse Prevention Program aimed at health care professionals. The authors provide information on the dynamics of battering relationships; ways health care workers can identify, assess, intervene, document, and refer battered women. Also included are sections on battering and pregnancy; signs of increasing danger; legal remedies; and community resources available to battered women. Several programs from various states that treat men who battter can be found on page 12.

Appendix A contains an extensive reference list of journal articles and books. Appendix B provides several articles related to abuse issues. Appendix C lists national and state information and resource centers.

Esposito, C.N. (1990). *Domestic violence: a guide for health care professionals* (3rd printing). Order from: Domestic Violence Prevention Program, Division on Women, N.J. Department of Community Affairs, 101 S. Broad Street, CN 801, Trenton, New Jersey 08625-0801, Attention: Nora Vista Shuda. (This manual is currently in the process of being revised to reflect the changes in the law. The revised edition will be available after January 1, 1992).

A comprehensive manual for use by nurses, physicians, social workers, and hospital security departments. It is further divided into two parts. Part I is a model protocol. The first section of the manual provides an introduction to the problem of wife abuse. The second section emphasizes a multidisciplinary approach to treating battered women. Discussions focus on crisis intervention techniques, the physical exam, confidentiality/privacy, documentation, photographing injuries, evidence collection and preservation, referrals, legal responsibilities of health care professionals, and the effects of imple-

menting a battered woman policy. The next section covers identification of adult victims of battering and elder abuse. The last section addresses the roles and responsibilities of various health care personnel from the emergency room secretarial staff to the public health nurse.

Part II offers a model curriculum for identification, treatment, and referral of adult victims of domestic violence. Suggestions are presented for speeches and audiovisuals. Topics under the model curriculum include the dynamics of domestic violence, definitions, an historical perspective, statistics, causes, and myths. Also included are community resources for battered women, types of protection/options available to victims under New Jersey law, presenting the protocol, group sessions, offering of a question & answer period, and type of summary & evaluation necessary to complete the course. The entire manual is 54 pages plus 29 pages of appendices.

Emergency Department, Maine Medical Center. (1990). *Identification, treatment, and referral of abused women.* To order a copy contact: Emmy L. Hunt, M.S.N., RN, CEN, Head Nurse, Department of Emergency Medicine, Maine Medical Center, 22 Bramhall Street, Portland, Maine 04102, (207) 871-4624.

The emergency department at Maine Medical Center implemented an abused woman protocol in 1990. Prior to implementation, all emergency department personnel attended educational sessions. The protocol uses a multidisciplinary approach to treating battered women. Included in this protocol are sections on identification of battered women; interventions specific to nursing, medicine, and social services; common injuries; documentation and photographing of injuries; privacy; danger assessment; safety plan; and referrals. The protocol is aimed primarily at emergency department personnel but can easily be adapted to other clinical settings.

Helton, A.S. (1987). *Protocol of care for the battered woman: Prevention of battering during pregnancy.* For ordering information contact: March of Dimes, Birth Defects Foundation, Professional Education Department, 1275 Mamaroneck Ave., White Plains, NY 10605, (914) 428-7100, or Anne Stewart Helton, RN, M.S., ACCE, Clinical Associate, Prevention of Battering During Pregnancy, Texas Woman's University, 1130 M.D. Anderson Blvd, Houston, TX 77030.

A guide primarily for nurses to detect pregnant women who are battered. This comprehensive manual provides: an overview of battering; specifics on battering and pregnancy; common indicators related to battering; a body map for indicating site of injury; abuse assessment tool written in English and Spanish; information on documenting in the medical record; and prevention strategies. The March of Dimes produced a video tape which can be used in conjunction with this protocol entitled, *Crime Against the Future.* The video tape can be rented or purchased. Contact the March of Dimes for further information.

55

Braham, R., Furniss, K., Holtz, H., and Stevens, M.E. (1986). *Hospital protocol on Domestic Violence.* They also authored, *Hospital training on domestic violence.* Both can be ordered from Jersey Battered Women's Services, Inc, 36 Elm Street, Morristown, NJ 07960.

The hospital protocol was written for use in the emergency department but is easily adaptable to other settings. The manual is comprehensive and quite specific. A multidisciplinary approach is used. The roles and responsibilities of nurses, physicians, social workers, etc. are given in detail. The manual is written in outline form and easy to follow. A short reference list of books, films journal articles, and publications is provided. The *Hospital Training on Domestic Violence* compliments the protocol manual. The entire curriculum requires a minimum of 3.5 hours. Included in the curriculum are specific behavioral objectives and outcomes; topics to be presented; method of instruction; evaluation mechanism; and materials needed.

Tomita, S., Clark, H., Williams, V., and Rabbitt, T. (1982). *Elder abuse and neglect protocol.* To obtain a copy contact: Karil Klingbeil, Department of Social Work, Harborview Medical Center, Seattle, WA, (206) 223-3000.

A comprehensive protocol for social workers but easily adaptable to other disciplines. This protocol includes: definitions of elder abuse/neglect; criteria for social worker involvement; type of information necessary for complete history and documentation of this information; assessment, diagnosis, and intervention strategies; desired outcome; and termination of social worker involvement. Attached to the protocol is a quality assurance checklist, and a copy of the *Goldfarb Dementia Scale.*

Rosenlieb, K.O. *The emergency department care of the sexual assault victim (RAPE).* Copies of the tape are available for a nominal fee. To order your copy contact: Kay O. Rosenlieb, RN, Ph.D., Chairperson Nursing Dept., Slippery Rock University, Slippery Rock, PA 16057.

This video tape was created and produced by Dr. Rosenlieb and three nursing students. The video tape highlights use of the rape evidence collection kit and the role of nursing. Dr. Rosenlieb uses the video in the Women's Health course.

WomanKind, Inc., Support systems for Battered Women. (1992). *WomanKind Emergency Department Protocol.* To obtain a copy contact: Susan M. Hadley, M.P.H., Founder and Executive Director, WomanKind, Fairview Southdale Hospital/Fairview Ridges Hospital, 6401 France Avenue south, Minneapolis, MN 55435. (612) 924-5775.

This is a comprehensive guide for healthcare professionals. It is designed primarily for use in the emergency department but is easily adaptable to any clinical setting. The protocol begins with a brief introduction, followed by a discussion of specific behaviors, common injuries/injury sites, and typical symptoms associated with battering. Section II provides more specific information on the interview process and treating not only the woman's physical injuries, but attending to her emotional needs as well. Privacy and confidentiality are the focus of Section III. Section IV elaborates on the importance of documenting the abuse history and any physical findings. The legal liabilities of health care professionals, procedures for photographing, and preservation of evidence are also discussed in this section. Section V contains a brief discussion about the correlation between substance abuse and domestic violence.

Each section provides sample questions necessary for obtaining and documenting a thorough history and physical findings. Also included with the WomanKind protocols is a list of The Battering Syndrome signs and symptoms; definition of terms related to battering with specific examples; and a bibliography.

Varvaro, F.F., and Cotman, P.B. (1986). *Domestic violence: A focus on the emergency room care of abused women.* To order a copy contact: Women's Center and Shelter of Greater Pittsburgh, P.O. box 9024, Pittsburgh, PA 15224. (412) 687-8017.

This comprehensive manual is written for emergency room personnel, but can be easily adapted to a variety of clinical settings. It is designed to be used as a classroom tool or for individual study. The manual begins with an Overview and Introduction which discusses the format (question and answer format); lists objectives; and defines terms used by the authors. The manual is further divided into four sections: Section I-Nursing Intervention; Section II-Shelter Intervention; Section III-Primary Intervention; and Section IV-Bibliography. Each section provides in-depth information necessary for the health care professional to identify, assess, intervene, document, and refer battered women. Sample questions and situations are provided as guidelines. Characteristics and other pertinent information pertaining to abusers are discussed. The bibliography is extensive and annotated. The manual concludes with an 11 question, short-answer post-test, including answers to the test.

REFERENCES

Campbell, J.C., and Sheridan, D.J. (1989). Emergency nursing interventions with battered women. *Journal of Emergency Nursing,* 15(1), 12–17.

Deckstein, L.J., and Nadelson, C.C. (1986). *Family Violence: Emergency issues of a national crisis.* Washington, D.C.: American Psychiatric Press, Inc.

Goldberg, W. and Tomlanovich, M.C. (1984). Domestic violence victims in the emergency department. *Journal of the American Medical Association,* 251(24), 3259–3264.

Helton, A.S., McFarlane, J., and Anderson, E. (1987). Battering during pregnancy: A prevalence study. *American Journal of Public Health,* 77(10), 1337–39.

Hilberman, E. (1980). Overview: The "wife-beater's wife" reconsidered. *American Journal of Psychiatry,* 137, 1336–1347.

Kurz, D., and Stark, E. (1988). Not-so-benign neglect: The medical response to battering. In K. Yllo & M. Bograd (Eds), *Feminist Perspectives on Wife Abuse.* Newbury Park, CA: Sage Publications, Inc.

McLeer, S.V. and Anwar, R. (1987). The role of the emergency physician in the prevention of domestic violence. *Annals of Emergency Medicine,* 16(10), 1155–1161.

McLeer, S.V. and Anwar, R. (1989). Education is not enough: A systems failure in protecting battered women. *Annals of Emergency Medicine*, 18(6), 651–653.

Randall, T. (1990). Domestic violence intervention calls for more than treating injuries. *Journal of the American Medical Association*, 264(8), 939–944.

Rosewater, L.B. (1988). Battered or schizophrenic? Psychological tests can't tell. In K. Yllo & M. Bograd (Eds), *Feminist Perspectives on Wife Abuse*. Newbury Park, CA: Sage Publications, Inc.

Stark, E., and Flitcraft, A. (1985). Woman-battering, child abuse and social heredity: What is the relationship? In N. Johnson (Ed), *Marital Violence*. Sociological Review Monograph #31. London: Routledge & Kegan Paul.

Stark, E., Flitcraft, A., and Frazier. (1979). Medicine and patriarchal violence: The social construction of a "Private" event. *International Journal of Health Services*, 9, 461–493.

Tilden, V.P., and Shepherd, P. (1987). Increasing the rate of identification of battered women in an emergency department: Use of a nursing protocol. *Research, Nursing and Health*, 10(4), 209–15.

Varvaro, F.F. (1989). Treatment of the battered woman: Effective response of the emergency department. *American College of Emergency Physicians*, 11, 8–9 & 13.

Wendy K. Taylor, M.S., RN, is Coordinator, Family Violence Program, Department of Medical Nursing and Social Service Department, at Rush-Presbyterian-St. Luke's Medical Center in Chicago. Jacquelyn C. Campbell, Ph.D, RN, FAAN, is Assistant Professor, Department of Community Health Nursing, at Wayne State University.

The Nursing Networking Violence Against Women (NNVAW) is a flexible coalition of nurses and other concerned individuals engaged in advocacy, research, clinical practice, and/or education on issues related to violence against women. For membership information ($10/year) and/or to submit suggestions for articles, write to Jackie Campbell, Wayne State University College of Nursing, Detroit, MI 48202. See Conference Report for announcement of the next NNVAW conference, May 17–19, 1991.

This article and others listing protocols can be found on the Response Data Base Disk.

Family Violence Program Grant Contributes to Prevention

A small grant from the Administration for Children and Families two years ago helped the New york State Coalition Against Domestic Violence respond to a request from women incarcerated in a New York facility and, in turn, generate other activities which are contributing to the prevention of family violence.

Gwen Wright, Director of the Coalition, explains that the HHS funds helped make it possible to hold a conference in response to a request from women at New York's Bedford Hills Correctional Facility. Incarcerated women involved in the project were participants in the facility's Family Violence Program, an innovative program that helps women understand the nature of violent and abusive behavior and enables them to build skills that will be needed when they return to their homes.

The women—imprisoned for crimes that had resulted from lifelong backgrounds of battering and other forms of abuse—wanted their Family Violence Program known about in other correctional facilities. Women in the program earlier had conducted an informal survey that indicated that as many as 65 percent of incarcerated women at the facility had been abused. Officials there believe the actual number is even higher.

Working in cooperation with the facility, the New York State Coalition Against Domestic Violence successfully applied for a grant which, in part, underwrote a conference at the Bedford Hills Facility. Participants at the conference in addition to the incarcerated women, included representatives from correctional facilities and coalitions in several states. As a result, a number of positive actions have occurred in the region.

One action that followed the conference was the establishment of a task force that is studying sexual assault issues throughout the state. Other initiatives included changes within the state's parole system. One of the most important results of the conference according to Sharon Smolick, who directs the program at Bedford Hills, is that it has raised consciousness about the problem throughout the region's correctional community.

A premise of the facility's program is that battered and sexually abused women who are incarcerated need program support comparable to that provided other women. The program at Bedford Hills has proved highly beneficial. "It's a good program," says Elaine Lord, Superintendent of the facility. "We're very pleased with it."

The discretionary grant funding for this activity, which was provided through the Family Violence Prevention and Services Act Program, was $12,000.

—Family Violence and Sexual Assault Bulletin

Notes

1. The Chilean study, for example, asked women whether they had experienced specific forms of behavior and then asked them to code the frequency of the behavior on a five-point ordinal scale ranging from 1 (all the time) to 5 (never). A woman was considered abused if her partner had ever used physical force against her beyond pushing, slapping, or throwing things—for example, if he had hit her with a fist (Larrain 1993).

2. These observations, published in an article in *Lancet* on the abuse of New Zealand women, are typical of the experience of most researchers: "In those reporting abuse during childhood, all recounted experiences involving genital contact, with most describing incidents of gross abuse. The great majority of those sexually assaulted in adult life had been the victims of rape or attempted rape. The physically abused group had all been subjected to unequivocal battery, with many suffering repeated injurious assaults. These women showed no tendencies to inflate minor incidents, but on the contrary, demonstrated a conservative approach in which only obvious assaults were labelled as abuse" (Mullen and others 1988).

3. These studies are all based on random probability samples of adult women interviewed in person or by telephone. All studies used legally grounded definitions of rape; thus, forms of penetration other than penile-vaginal are included, and women were not instructed to exclude rape by their husbands. Questions were typically framed to explicitly define the behaviors that should be included in the definition—for example: "Has a man made you have sex by using force or threatening to harm you? When we use the word sex we mean a man putting his penis in your vagina even if he didn't ejaculate (come)." This is followed by: "If he did not try to put his penis in your vagina, has a man made you do other sexual things like oral sex or anal sex, or put fingers or objects inside you by using force or threatening to harm you?"

4. In evaluating the sources of variability in prevalence of sexual abuse, Peters, Wyatt, and Finkelhor (1986) suggest that differences in definitions and methods used in these studies probably account for most of the variations reported. The operational definitions of abuse varied according to whether they include contact or noncontact violations, or both, the nature of the violations, the age of the girl at the time of abuse, and the difference in age between the perpetrator and the victim. Most definitions include contact and noncontact abuse, include respondents 17 and under (or sometimes 15 and under), and use an age difference of five years (Peters, Wyatt, and Finkelhor 1986). When Wyatt's (1985) study, which reported a 62 percent rate of prevalence, was recomputed to exclude peer experiences (and thus to conform to the definition used by Russell and Finkelhor), the prevalence rate decreased to 53 percent, almost matching Russell's 54 percent finding (1983). Finkelhor's (1979) study, which found 19 percent prevalence, used a self-administered questionnaire, while the others used face-to-face interviews. The definition used in these studies includes all types of intrafamilial contact abuse. For abuse that occurs outside the family, it includes all types of contact abuse up to age 13, but only completed or attempted forcible rapes for ages 14 to 17.

5. The survey measured sexual abuse using a series of questions that asked about sexual contact between a child and his or her parent, stepparent, or parental partner, including breast or genital touching, or sexual intercourse that occurred before age 16 with an individual more than five years his or her senior. Also included was any forced sexual contact regardless of age. Respondents were asked to complete an anonymous survey questionnaire that was placed in a sealed envelope and dropped into a bag containing at least six other questionnaires.

6. It may be that rapes of young girls are reported more often, but in the United States at least, this is not the case: girls under 18 are less likely than older women to report their assault (U.S. Congress 1990).

7. A recent analysis of national demographic data from China contends that underreporting of female births and an increase in prenatal sex selection through ultrasound and selective abortion can explain almost all the increase in the reported sex ratio at birth in China during the late 1980s, ruling out the possibility of widespread female infanticide (Zeng, Tu, and Gu 1993).

8. China manufactured its first ultrasound machine in 1979, and by the end of the 1980s it was making 10,000 and importing more than 2,000 each year. A Chinese demographer estimates that 100,000 ultrasound scanners were in place around the country by 1990. One study reported that all of the peasants interviewed—even those with no schooling and living in remote regions—knew that there was a device that could determine the sex of a fetus (Kristof 1993).

9. Sen originally estimated that more than 100 million women were missing. In a detailed recalculation, however, Princeton demographer Ansley Coale estimated that the true number of missing women was closer to 60 million in the 1980s (in countries including Bangladesh, China, Egypt, India, Nepal, and Pakistan, and in West Asia). According to Coale, Sen's estimate used an inappropriate comparison that failed to take into account the loss of male lives in the west due to war and an age composition that reflected past low fertility. Coale's revised estimate adjusts for these factors (Coale 1991).

10. In the United States in 1980, 20 million people were on a "serious" diet at any one moment (*Harvard Medical School Health Letter* 1980). Dieters spent more than $10 billion that year on efforts to lose weight (Chernin 1981).

11. Post-traumatic stress disorder (PTSD) is a complex of symptoms seen in the aftermath of extreme trauma. It is characterized by intrusive memories, hyperarousal alternating with psychological numbing and withdrawal, and attempts to avoid any reminders of the trauma.

12. A recent study by the Addiction Research Foundation in Toronto found that battered women use sedatives 74 percent more and sleeping pills 40.5 percent more than women who are not battered (Groenveld and Shain 1989).

13. The World Health Organization defines maternal mortality as a death during pregnancy or within 42 days afterward, from causes related to or aggravated by the pregnancy or its management.

14. Although male approval is by no means always the greatest determinant of contraceptive use, see Gallen 1986 and Kincaid and others 1991 for examples of cases where it is.

15. Variables controlled for include years in legal or common-law union during previous five years, raised in lower-class home, education of mother, education of father, raised in stable nuclear family, raised solely by mother, raised with a stepfather, degree of affection mother's partner showed her, degree of physical and emotional abuse to mother, degree of affection mother showed son, degree of affection mother's partner showed son, degree to which mother's partner physically and emotionally abused son, man's educational status, and man's occupational status.

16. The Davis and Carlson (1987) study found that 90 percent of abused boys and 75 percent of those witnessing violence (compared with 13 percent for controls) had behavior problem scores greater than one standard deviation above the norm.

17. The women's police station in Argentina was eliminated in 1993, apparently due to lack of political support. But by the end of 1992 Colombia had 60 special stations, and Peru had added four new women's units in Lima (ISIS International 1993).

18. A study in Punta Arenas, Chile, that cross-checked hospital records with local police records found that of 736 cases of violence against women registered between 1988 and 1989 at the Regional Hospital and Clinica Magallanes, only 15.4 percent were also registered at the local police court. These findings underscore the importance of using health facilities to identify and refer victims of violence (Ojeda and Perez 1992).

19. In addition, few violence prevention programs have been systematically evaluated. A survey sponsored by the Carnegie Council on Adolescent Development of 83 teen violence prevention programs in the United States found that, although they were geared toward teen violence, many focused on elementary school-age children or early adolescents. Of the 51 programs reviewed, only 21 percent evaluated outcomes, generally through simple measures of the pre- and post-test attitudes and knowledge of participants. Only a handful have been evaluated at a level approaching rigorous experimental design. But less formal evaluations indicate that some of the programs hold great promise (Wilson-Brewer and others 1991).

20. Between 1984 and 1989 arrests for minor assaults in the United States increased 70 percent, largely because of new "presumptive-arrest" policies and mandatory arrest laws for domestic violence (Schmidt and Sherman 1993).

21. One potentially important finding is the positive effect that issuing arrest warrants appears to have on batterers who left the scene before the police arrived. In a study in Omaha absent offenders who were randomly assigned to receive a warrant were less violent at follow-up than those who did not receive a warrant (Dunford, Huizinga, and Elliot 1990). Because more than half of all offenders leave the scene before the police arrive, this intervention may have more impact on rates of recidivism than any strategy targeting perpetrators who are present at the scene (Schmidt and Sherman 1993).

22. Studies show that about a third of violent men can be expected to remain violence-free one to three years after a violent incident even without treatment or legal intervention (Rosenfeld 1992).

Bibliography

Acasadi, George, and Gwendolyn Johnson-Acasadi. 1990. "Safe Motherhood in South Asia: Sociocultural and Demographic Aspects of Maternal Health." Background paper prepared for Safe Motherhood South Asia Conference, Lahore, Pakistan, March 24-28.

Adamson, Peter. 1988. "Two Powerful Sources for Child Survival." *People* 15(1).

Agnes, Flavia. 1988. "Violence in the Family: Wife Beating." In R. Ghadially, editor, *Women in Indian Society*. New Delhi: Sage Publications.

Amaro, Hortensia, Lise Fried, Howard Cabral, and Barry Zuckerman. 1990. "Violence during Pregnancy and Substance Use." *American Journal of Public Health* 80(5):575-79.

Americas Watch. 1991. "Criminal Injustice: Violence against Women in Brazil." Human Rights Watch, The Women's Rights Project, New York.

Aminata, Maiga Ka. 1984. "Early Childhood Marriage in Senegal." In *Traditional Practices Affecting the Health of Women and Children in Africa*. Dakar, Senegal.

Anderson, Jessie, Judy Martin, Paul Mullen, and Sarah Romans-Clarkson. Forthcoming. "Violence against Women in New Zealand: The Otago Women's Health Survey." *Journal of the American Academy of Child and Adolescent Psychiatry*.

APDC (Asian and Pacific Development Center). 1989. *Asian and Pacific Women's Resource and Action Series: Health.* Kuala Lumpur.

Archavanitkui, Kritaya, and Anthony Pramualratana. 1990. "Factors Affecting Women's Health in Thailand." Paper presented at the Workshop on Women's Health in Southeast Asia, Population Council, Jakarta, October 29-31.

Asia Pacific Forum on Women, Law and Development. 1990. *My Rights, Who Controls?* Kuala Lumpur.

Australia, Department of the Prime Minister and Cabinet Office of the Status of Women. 1991. *National Committee on Violence against Women: Position Paper.* Canberra: Australian Government Publishing Service.

Avendano, Cecilia, and Jorge Vergara. 1992. "La Violencia Sexual en Chile, Dimensiones: Colectiva, Cultural y Política." Servicio Nacional de la Mujer, Santiago, Chile.

Avery, Byllye. 1990. "Breathing Life into Ourselves: The Evolution of the National Black Women's Health Project." In E.C. White, editor, *The Black Women's Health Book.* Seattle: Seal Press.

Badgely, R.F. 1984. *Sexual Offenses against Children: Report of the Committee on Sexual Offenses against Children and Youth.* Volume 1. Ottawa: Canadian Publishing Centre.

Banwell, Suzanna Stout. 1990. "Law, Status of Women and Family Planning in Sub-Saharan Africa: A Suggestion for Action." The Pathfinder Fund, Nairobi.

Barragan Alvarado, Lourdes, Alexandra Ayala Marin, and Gloria Camacho Zambrano. 1992. "Proyecto Educativo Sobre Violencia de Género en la Relación Doméstica de Pareja." Centro de Planificación y Estudios Sociales (CEPLAES), Quito, Ecuador.

Batres, Gioconda. 1993. Executive Director, Ser y Crecer. Personal communication. San José, Costa Rica, March 18.

Beattie, Valerie. 1992. "Analysis of the Results of a Survey on Sexual Violence in the UK." Women's Forum, Cambridge, U.K.

Becker, J.V., L.J. Skinner, G.G. Abel, and J. Chicon. 1986. "Level of Postassault Sexual Functioning in Rape and Incest Victims." *Archives of Sexual Behavior* 15:37-49.

Becker, J.V., L.J. Skinner, G.G. Abel, and E.C. Treacy. 1982. "Incidence and Types of Sexual Dysfunctions in Rape and Incest Victims." *Journal of Sex and Marital Therapy* 8:65-74.

Beneria, Lourdes, and Martha Roldan. 1987. *The Crossroads of Class and Gender*. Chicago: University of Chicago Press.

Berenguer, Ana Maria. 1988. "Alternativas Desde la Medicina Legal y Experiéncias Sobre la Violencia Intrafamilar." In *Violencia en la Intimidad.* Bogata, Colombia: Corporación Casa de la Mujer.

Bernard, Cheryl. 1986. "Patterns of Violence against Women in the Family." Background document prepared for the Expert Group Meeting on Violence in the Family with a Special Emphasis on Its Effects on Women, Vienna, Austria. United Nations, New York. BAW/EGM/86/wp.1.

Bhatia, Shushum. 1985. "Status and Survival." *World Health* (April):12-14.

Blane, H.T., B.A. Miller, and K.E. Leonard. 1988. *Intra- and Intergenerational Aspects of Serious Domestic Violence and Alcohol and Drugs.* Washington, D.C.: National Institute of Justice.

Blumberg, R.L. 1989. *Making the Case for the Gender Variable: Women and the Wealth and Well-Being of Nations.* Technical Reports in Gender and Development 2. Washington, D.C.: U.S. Agency for International Development, Office of Women and Development.

Bobadilla, Jose. 1993. World Development Report project team. Personal communication. World Bank, Washington, D.C.

Bograd, Michele. 1984. "Family Systems Approach to Wife Battering: A Feminist Critique." *American Journal of Orthopsychiatry* 54:558-68.

Boyer, Debra, and David Fine. 1992. "Sexual Abuse as a Factor in Adolescent Pregnancy and Child Maltreatment." *Family Planning Perspectives* 24(1):4-10.

Bradley, Christine. 1988. "How Can We Help Rural Beaten Wives? Some Suggestions from Papua New Guinea." Paper presented at the International Welsh Women's Aid Conference, Cardiff, Wales.

———. 1990. "Why Male Violence against Women is a Development Issue: Reflections from Papua New Guinea." Draft UNIFEM Occasional Paper. United Nations Fund for Women, New York.

Breslau, N., G.C. Davis, P. Andreski, and E. Peterson. 1991. "Traumatic Events and Posttraumatic Stress Disorder in an Urban Population of Young Adults." *Archives of General Psychiatry* 48:216-22.

Briere, John, and M. Runtz. 1987. "Post Sexual Abuse Trauma: Data and Implications for Clinical Practice." *Journal of Interpersonal Violence* 2:367-79.

"Britain: Marital Rape Exemption to Be Outlawed." 1990. *New York Times,* December 28.

Browne, Angela. 1987. *When Battered Women Kill.* New York: Free Press.

Browne, Angela, and David Finkelhor. 1986. "The Impact of Child Sexual Abuse: A Review of the Research." *Psychological Bulletin* 99:66-77.

Browne, Angela, and Kirk Williams. 1992. "Resource Availability for Women at Risk and Partner Homicide." *Law and Society Review* 23(1):75.

Brumberg, Joan Jacobs. 1988. *Fasting Girls: The Emergence of Anorexia Nervosa as a Modern Disease.* Cambridge, Mass.: Harvard University Press.

Bruynooghe, R., and others. 1989. "Study of Physical and Sexual Violence against Belgian Women." Department of Sciences Humaines et Sociales, Limburgs Universitair Centrum, Belgium. As cited in Ada Garcia, "Sexual Violence against Women: Contribution to a Strategy for Countering the Various Forms of Such Violence in the Council of Europe Member States." European Committee for Equality between Women and Men, Strasbourg, France, 1991.

Bullock, Linda F., and Judith McFarlane. 1989. "The Birth Weight/Battering Connection." *American Journal of Nursing* 89(9):1153-55.

Bullock, Linda, Judith McFarlane, Louise Bateman, and Virginia Miller. 1989. "The Prevalence and Characteristics of Battered Women in a Primary Care Setting." *Nurse Practitioner* 14:47-54.

Burgess, A.W., and L.L. Holmstrom. 1979. "Adaptive Strategies and Recovery from Rape." *American Journal of Psychiatry* 136:1278-82.

Burnam, M. Audrey, Judith A. Stein, J.M. Golding, J.M. Siegel, S.B. Sorenson, A.B. Forsythe, and C.A. Telles. 1988. "Sexual Assault and Mental Disorders in a Community Population." *Journal of Consulting and Clinical Psychology* 56(6):843-50.

Busto, Miren Aduncion. 1991. "BDZ: La Tranquila Adicción de Santiago." Santiago, Chile: Corporacion de Salud y Politicas Sociales.

Cahill, C., S.P. Llewelyn, and C. Pearson. 1991. "Long-term Effects of Sexual Abuse which Occurred in Childhood: A Review." *British Journal of Clinical Psychology* 30:117-30.

Caldwell, J.C. 1979. "Education as a Factor in Mortality Decline: An Examination of Nigerian Data." *Population Studies* 33(3):395-413.

Campbell, Jacquelyn. 1986. "Nursing Assessment for Risk of Homicide in Battered Women." *American Nursing Society* 8:36-51.

Campbell, Jacquelyn, and Peggy Alford. 1989. "The Dark Consequences of Marital Rape." *American Journal of Nursing* (July):946-48.

CAMVAC (Centro de Apoyo A Mujeres Violadas). 1985. "Carpeta de Información Básica Para la Atención Solidaria y Feminista a Mujeres Violadas." Mexico City.

Canada, Government of. 1991. "New Family Violence Initiative Underway." *Canadian Women's Studies, Violence against Women: Strategies for Change* 12(1):111.

Canada, House of Commons. 1991. *The War against Women.* Report of the Standing Committee on Health and Welfare, Social Affairs, Seniors and the Status of Women. Ottawa.

Canada, Solicitor General. 1985. "Female Victims of Crime." Canadian Urban Victimization Survey Bulletin 4. Programs Branch/Research and Statistics Group, Ottawa.

Canadian Centre for Justice Statistics. 1988. *Homicide in Canada 1987: A Statistical Perspective.* Ottawa: Ministry of Supply and Services.

Carcedo, Anna. 1993. Director, CEFEMINA. Personal communication. San Jose, Costa Rica, March 15.

Carrillo, Roxanna. 1992. *Battered Dreams: Violence against Women as an Obstacle to Development.* New York: United Nations Fund for Women.

Casey, Maeve. 1988. "Domestic Violence against Women: The Women's Perspective." Dublin, Ireland: Federation of Women's Refugees.

Castillo, Delia, Maria Batres, Ofelia Rosales, and Janeth Alvarez. 1992. "Violencia Hacia La Mujer en Guatemala." Paper presented at the First Central American Seminar on Violence against Women as a Public Health Problem, Managua, Nicaragua, March 11-13.

Center for Women's Global Leadership. 1992. *Women, Violence and Human Rights.* New Brunswick, N.J.: Rutgers University.

———. 1993. Personal communication. New Brunswick, N.J.

Chacon, K., F. Herrera, A.M. Rojas, and M. Villalobos. 1990. "Características de La Mujer Agredida Atendida en el Patronato Nacional de la Infancia (PANI)." San José, Costa Rica. As cited in Gioconda Batres and Cecilia Claramunt, *La Violencia Contra La Mujer En La Familia Costarricense: Un Problema de Salud Pública,* San José, Costa Rica: ILANUD, 1992.

Chatterjee, Meera. 1990. *Indian Women: Their Health and Economic Productivity.* World Bank Discussion Paper 109. Washington, D.C.

Chen, Lincoln, Emdadul Huq, and Stan D'Souza. 1981. "Sex Bias in the Family Allocation of Food and Health Care in Rural Bangladesh." *Population and Development Review* 7(1):55-70.

Chernin, Kim. 1981. *The Obsession: Reflections on the Tyranny of Slender.* New York: Harper and Row.

Claramunt, Cecelia. 1991. "Características de la población atendida en el programa de atención amor sin agresión (julio 1990-1991)." San José, Costa Rica. As cited in Gioconda Batres and Cecilia Claramunt, *La Violencia Contra La Mujer En La Familia Costarricense: Un Problema de Salud Pública,* San Jose, Costa Rica: ILANUD, 1992.

Clay, Jason W., and others. *The Spoils of Famine: Ethiopian Famine Policy and Peasant Agriculture.* Cultural Survival Report 25. Cambridge, Mass.: Cultural Survival, Inc.

Coale, Ansley. 1991. "Excess Female Mortality and the Balance of the Sexes in the Population: An Estimate of the Number of Missing Females." *Population and Development Review* 17(3):517-23.

Coale, Ansley, and Judith Banister. 1992. "High Ratios of Males to Females in the Population of China." Paper presented at the International Seminar on China's 1990 Population Census, Beijing, October 19-23. Princeton University, Princeton, N.J., and U.S. Census Bureau, China Branch, Washington, D.C.

Consumers Association of Penang. 1988. *Rape in Malaysia.* Penang, Malaysia.

Cook, Rebecca, and Deborah Maine. 1987. "Spousal Veto over Family Planning Services." *American Journal of Public Health* 77(3):339-44.

Council of Europe. 1986. Recommendation no. R.85.4 of the Committee of Ministers, adopted March 26, 1986.

Council on Scientific Affairs, American Medical Association. 1992. "Violence against Women: Relevance for Medical Practitioners." *Journal of the American Medical Association* 267(23):3184-89.

Counts, Dorothy. 1987. "Female Suicide and Wife Abuse: A Cross-Cultural Perspective." *Suicide and Life Threatening Behavior* 17(3):194-205.

Counts, Dorothy Ayers, Judith Brown, and Jacquelyn Campbell, editors. 1992. *Sanctions and Sanctuary: Cultural Perspectives on the Beating of Wives.* Boulder, Colo.: Westview Press.

COVAC (Colectivo de Lucha Contra La Violencia Hacia Las Mujeres). 1990. "Evaluación de Proyecto para Educación, Capacitación, y Atención a Mujeres y Menores de Edad en Materia de Violencia Sexual, Enero a Diciembre 1990." Asociación Mexicana Contra la Violencia a las Mujeres, Mexico City.

Croll, Elizabeth. 1980. *Feminism and Socialism in China.* New York: Schocken Publishers.

Das Gupta, Monica. 1987. "Selective Discrimination against Children in Rural Punjab, India." *Population and Development Review* 13(1):95-111.

Datinguinoo, Vinia M. 1991. "Battered Lives: An Interview with Raquel Edralin Tiglao." *Marhia* (Institute for Social Studies and Action, Quezon City, Philippines) 4(3):1-7.

Dattel, Bonnie. 1992. Associate Professor and Director of Research and Education in Division of Maternal and Fetal Medicine, Eastern Virginia Medical School, Norfolk, Virginia. Personal communication. March 14.

Davis, Liane V., and Bonnie Carlson. 1987. "Observation of Spouse Abuse: What Happens to the Children?" *Journal of Interpersonal Violence* 2(3):278-91.

DeKeseredy, Walter, and Katherine Kelly. 1993. Personal communication. Preliminary data from First National Study on Dating Violence in Canada. Family Violence Prevention Division, Department of Health and Welfare, Ottawa, Canada.

Dembo, R. 1987. "Physical Abuse, Sexual Victimization and Illicit Drug Use: A Structural Analysis among High-Risk Adolescents." *Journal of Adolescence* 10:13-33.

Dimenstein, Gilberto. 1992. "Pais conta 337 mulheres agredidas por dia." *Folha de San Paulo,* November 29.

Dixon-Mueller, Ruth. 1993. "The Sexuality Connection in Reproductive Health." *Studies in Family Planning* 24(5):269-82.

Dobash, Russel, R. Emerson Dobash, Margo Wilson, and Martin Daly. 1992. "The Myth of Sexual Symmetry in Marital Violence." *Social Problems* 39(1):71-91.

Domestic Violence Research Group. 1993. "A Study on Violence Precipitated by Husbands (Boyfriends) in Japan: Preliminary Findings." Paper presented at the NGO parallel activities at the United Nations World Conference on Human Rights, Vienna, Austria, June 12-25.

Dorkenoo, Efua, and Elworthy Scilla. 1992. *Female Genital Mutilation: Proposals for Change.* London: Minority Rights Group.

Drossman, D.A., J. Leserman, G. Nachman, Z.M. Li, H. Gluck, T.C. Toomey, and C.M. Mitchell. 1990. "Sexual and Physical Abuse in Women with Functional or Organic Gastrointestinal Disorders." *Annals of Internal Medicine* 113:828-33.

Dunford, Franklyn, David Huizinga, and Delbert Elliot. 1990. "The Role of Arrest in Domestic Assault: The Omaha Police Experiment." *Criminology* 28(2):183-206.

Economic and Social Council. 1992. "Report of the Working Group on Violence against Women." United Nations, Vienna. E/CN.6/WG.2/1992/L.3.

Edleson, J.L., and R.J. Grusznski. 1988. "Treating Men Who Batter: Four Years of Outcome Data from the Domestic Abuse Project." *Journal of Social Service Research* 12:3-22.

Ellman, Annie. 1993. Director, Brooklyn Anti-Violence Education Project. Personal communication. February 11.

Etue, Elizabeth. 1991. "Communities and Schools: A Blueprint for the Future." *Canadian Woman Studies, Violence against Women: Strategies for Change* 12(1):90-91.

Facio, Alda. 1993. Personal communication. Programa Mujer, Justicia y Genero, ILANUD, San Jose, Costa Rica.

Family Violence Prevention Fund. 1993. *Health Alert: Medical Care System's Response to Domestic Violence* 1(1) (San Francisco, California).

Fauveau, Vincent, and Therese Blanchet. 1989. "Deaths from Injuries and Induced Abortion among Rural Bangladeshi Women." *Social Science and Medicine* 29(9):1121-28.

Felitti, V.J. 1991. "Long-term Medical Consequences of Incest, Rape and Molestation." *Southern Medical Journal* 84:328-31.

Fernandez, Irene. 1992. "Mobilizing on All Fronts: A Comprehensive Strategy to End Violence against Women." In Margaret Schuler, editor, *Freedom from Violence.* New York: UNIFEM.

Fernando, Nimalka. 1993. Personal communication. Asia Pacific Forum on Women Law and Development, Kuala Lumpur, Malaysia.

Fildes, John, Laura Reed, and Nancy Jones. 1992. "Trauma: The Leading Cause of Maternal Death." *Journal of Trauma* 32:643-45.

Finklehor, David. 1979. *Sexually Victimized Children.* New York: Free Press.

———. 1987. "The Sexual Abuse of Children: Current Research Reviewed." *Psychiatric Annals* 17:233-41.

Finklehor, David, and Kersti Yllo. 1985. *License to Rape: Sexual Abuse of Wives.* New York: Holt, Rinehart, and Winston.

Flanagan, T.J., and E.F. McGarrell. 1986. *Sourcebook of Criminal Justice Statistics—1985 (NCJ-100899).* Washington, D.C.: U.S. Department of Justice, Bureau of Justice Statistics.

Flavia d'Oliveira, Ana. 1993. "Violence against Women as a Public Health Issue." Paper presented at the Second World Conference on Injury Control, Atlanta, Georgia, May 20-23.

Foa, E.B., B. Olasov, and G.S. Steketee. 1987. "Treatment of Rape Victims." Paper presented at conference on State of the Art in Sexual Assault, Charleston, South Carolina, September.

Folch-Lyon, Evelyn, Luis Macorra, and S. Bruce Schearer. 1981. "Focus Group and Survey Research on Family Planning in Mexico." *Studies in Family Planning* 12(12):409-32.

Fort, A.L. 1989. "Investigation of the Social Context of Fertility and Family Planning: A Qualitative Study in Peru." *International Family Planning Perspectives* 15(3):88-94.

Frieze, Irene, and Angela Browne. 1989. "Violence in Marriage." In Lloyd Ohlin and Michael Tonry, editors, *Family Violence.* Crime and Justice Series 11. Chicago: University of Chicago Press.

Fullilove, M.T., E.A. Lown, and R.E. Fullilove. 1992. "Crack 'Hos and Skeezers: Traumatic Experiences of Women Crack Users." *Journal of Sex Research* 29(2):275-87.

Gallen, M.A. 1986. "Men—New Focus for Family Planning Programs." Population Reports Series J, No. 33. Johns Hopkins School of Hygiene and Public Health, Population Information Program, Baltimore, Md.

Garcia, Ana Isabel. 1992. *Mujeres Latinoamericanas en Cifras: Guatemala.* Madrid, Spain: Ministerio de Asuntos Sociales, Instituto de la Mujer.

Gartner, Rosemary, and Bill McCarthy. 1991. "The Social Distribution of Femicide in Urban Canada, 1921-1988." *Law and Society Review* 25(2):287-311.

Gavey, Nicola. 1991. "Sexual Victimization Prevalence among New Zealand University Students." *Journal of Consulting and Clinical Psychology* 59:464-66.

Gelles, Richard. 1993. "Constraints against Family Violence: How Well Do They Work?" *American Behavioral Scientist* 36(5):575-86.

George, Sabu, Rajaratnam Abel, and Barbara Miller. 1992. "Female Infanticide in Rural South India." *Economic and Political Weekly,* May 30.

Gibson, M.A. 1990. "Equity for Female Teachers: A National Survey of Employment, Training and Promotional Opportunities for Community School Teachers in Papua New Guinea." Report 65 of the National Research Institute, Educational Research Division, Waigani. Draft.

Golding, Jacqueline, Judith Stein, Judith Siegel, M. Audrey Burnam, and Susan Sorenson. 1988. "Sexual Assault History and Use of Health and Mental Health Services." *American Journal of Community Psychology* 16(5):625-44.

Gordon, Margaret T., and Stephanie Riger. 1989. *The Female Fear.* New York: Free Press.

Gordon, Richard. 1990. *Anorexia and Bulimia: Anatomy of a Social Epidemic.* Cambridge, Mass.: Basil Blackwell.

Graitcer, Philip. 1994. Personal communication. Emory School of Public Health, Atlanta, Georgia.

Graitcer, Philip, and Z. Youssef, editors. 1993. *Injury in Egypt: An Analysis of Injuries as a Health Problem.* Washington, D.C.: U.S. Agency for International Development; and Cairo: Ministry of Health.

Grant, Robert, Michael Preda, and J. David Martin. 1989. "Domestic Violence in Texas: A Study of Statewide and Rural Spouse Abuse." Midwestern State University, Bureau of Business and Government Research, Wichita Falls, Texas.

Griffiths, Marcia. 1988. "Maternal Self-Confidence and Child Well-Being." Paper presented at the Society for Applied Anthropology Annual Meeting, Tampa, Florida, April 20-24. Manoff Group, Washington, D.C.

Grisso, Jeane, and others. 1991. "A Population-Based Study of Injuries of Inner-City Women." *American Journal of Epidemiology* 134(1):59-68.

Groenveld, J., and M. Shain. 1989. *Drug Abuse among Victims of Physical and Sexual Abuse: A Preliminary Report.* Toronto: Addiction Research Foundation.

Haffejee, Ismail E. 1991. "Sexual Abuse of Indian (Asian) Children in South Africa: First Report in a Community Undergoing Cultural Change." *Child Abuse and Neglect* 15:147-51.

Handwerker, Penn. 1993a. "Gender Power Differences between Parents and High-Risk Sexual Behavior by Their Children: AIDS/STD Risk Factors Extend to a Prior Generation." *Journal of Women's Health* 2(3):301.

———. 1993b. "Power, Gender Violence, and High-Risk Sexual Behavior: AIDS/STD Risk Factors Need to Be Defined More Broadly." Personal communication. Humboldt State University, Department of Anthropology, Arcata, California, February 10.

Hanson, R.K. 1990. "Psychiatric Impacts of Sexual Abuse and Assault." *Annals of Sex Research* 3:187-232.

Harrel, Adele. 1991. "Evaluation of Court-Ordered Treatment for Domestic Violence Offenders." The Urban Institute, Washington, D.C.

Harvard Medical School Health Letter 41(2), December 1980.

Haskell, Lori, and Melanie Randall. 1993. "The Women's Safety Project: Summary of Key Statistical Findings." Canadian Panel on Violence against Women, Ottawa.

Haynes, R.H. 1984. "Suicide in Figi: A Preliminary Study." *British Journal of Psychiatry* 145:433-38.

Hedley, Rodney, and Efua Dorkenoo. 1992. *Child Protection and Female Genital Mutilation: Advice for Health, Education, and Social Work Professionals.* London: FOWARD, Ltd.

Heise, Lori. 1989. "International Dimensions of Violence against Women." *Response* 12(1):3-11.

———. 1991. "When Women Are Prey." *Washington Post,* December 13.

———. 1993. "Violence against Women: The Missing Agenda." In Marge Koblinsky, Judith Timyan, and Jill Gay, editors, *Women's Health: A Global Perspective.* Boulder, Colo.: Westview Press.

Heise, Lori, and Jane Roberts Chapman. 1992. "Reflections on a Movement: The U.S. Battle against Woman Abuse." In Margaret Schuler, editor, *Freedom from Violence: Women's Strategies from around the World.* Washington, D.C.: OEF International.

Helton, Anne, Judith McFarlane, and E. Anderson. 1987. "Battered and Pregnant: A Prevalence Study." *American Journal of Public Health* 77:1337-39.

Herman, Judith. 1992. *Trauma and Recovery.* New York: Basic Books.

Hosken, Fran. 1988. "International Seminar: Female Circumcision Strategies to Bring about Change." *Women's International Network News* 14(3):24-37.

Hull, Terence. 1990. "Recent Trends in Sex Ratios at Birth in China." *Population and Development Review* 16(1):63-83.

Human Rights Watch. 1992. *Double Jeopardy: Police Abuse of Women in Pakistan.* New York.

Hyman, Batya. 1993. "Economic Consequences of Child Sexual Abuse in Women." Ph.D. dissertation. Brandeis University, Heller School of Policy, Waltham, Mass.

Isaac, Nancy, and Ricardo Sanchez. 1992. "Emergency Department Response to Battered Women in Massachusetts." Paper presented at the American Public Health Association Conference, Washington, D.C., November.

ISIS International. 1988. "Campana sobre la violencia en contra de la mujer." *Boletín* (ISIS International, Red de Salud de las Mujeres Latinoamericanas y del Caribe, Santiago, Chile) April:16-17.

———. 1990. *Violencia en Contra de la Mujer en America Latina y El Caribe.* Santiago, Chile.

———. 1993. "Legislación Sobre Violencia Doméstica y Sexual." *Boletín* (Red Feminista Latinoamericana y del Caribe Contra La Violencia Doméstica y Sexual, Santiago, Chile) 1.

Jaffe, P., D. Wolfe, S. Wilson, and L. Zack. 1986. "Similarities in Behavioral and Social Maladjustment among Child Victims and Witnesses to Family Violence." *American Journal of Orthopsychiatry* 56:142-46.

James, J., and J. Meyerding. 1977. "Early Sexual Experience and Prostitution." *American Journal of Psychiatry* 134:1381-85.

Jellinek, M., Michael Murphy, and Francis Poitrast. 1992. "Serious Child Maltreatment in Massachusetts: The Course of 206 Children through the Courts." *Child Abuse and Neglect* 16(2):179-85.

Johnson, Holly. 1989. "Wife Assault in Canada." Paper presented at the Annual Meeting of the American Society of Criminology.

Karkal, Malini. 1985. "How the Other Half Dies in Bombay." *Economic and Political Weekly,* August 24, p. 1424.

Kauffman, J., and E. Zigler. 1987. "Do Abused Children Become Abusive Parents?" *American Journal of Orthopsychiatry* 57:186-92.

Kelkar, Govind. 1992. "Stopping the Violence against Women: Issues and Perspectives from India." In Margaret Schuler, editor, *Freedom from Violence: Strategies from around the World.* Washington, D.C.: OEF International.

Kellermann, A.L., and J.A. Mercy. 1992. "Men, Women, and Murder: Gender-Specific Differences in Rates of Fatal Violence and Victimization." *Journal of Trauma* 33(4):1-5.

Kennedy, L.W., and D.G. Dutton. 1989. "The Incidence of Wife Assault in Alberta." *Canadian Journal of Behavioral Science* 21:40-54.

Kerns, Virginia. 1992. "Preventing Violence against Women: A Central American Case." In Counts, Brown, and Campbell 1992.

Khanna, Renu. 1992. Personal communication. Social Action for Rural and Tribal Inhabitants of India (SARTHI). Baroda, Gujurat State, India.

Kilpatrick, Dean. 1988. "Rape Aftermath Symptom Test." In M. Hersen and A.S. Bellack, editors, *Dictionary of Behavioral Assessment Techniques.* New York: Pergamon Press.

———. 1990. "Testimony before the House Select Committee on Children, Youth, and Families." As cited by Congressional Caucus for Women's Issues, "Violence against Women Fact Sheet," Washington, D.C., 1990.

Kilpatrick, D.G., C.N. Edmunds, and A.K. Seymour. 1992. *Rape in America: A Report to the Nation.* Arlington, Va.: The National Victim Center.

Kim, Kwang-iei, and Young-gyu Cho. 1992. "Epidemiological Survey of Spousal Abuse in Korea." In Emilio C. Viano, editor, *Intimate Violence: Interdisciplinary Perspectives.* Washington, D.C.: Hemisphere Publishing Corporation.

Kincaid, D. Lawrence, and others. 1991. "Family Planning and the Empowerment of Women in Bangladesh." Paper presented at the 119th Annual Meeting of the American Public Health Association, Atlanta, November 13.

Kirk, Robin. 1993. *Untold Terror: Violence against Women in Peru's Armed Conflict.* New York: Human Rights Watch.

Kisekka, Mere, and B. Otesanya. 1988. "Sexually Transmitted Disease as a Gender Issue: Examples from Nigeria and Uganda." Paper given at the AFARD/AAWORD Third General Assembly on the African Crisis and the Women's Vision of the Way Out, Dakar, August.

Korea Sexual Violence Relief Center. 1991. "Information Booklet." Seoul.

Koss, Mary P. 1990. "The Women's Mental Health Research Agenda: Violence against Women." *American Psychologist* 45(3):374-80.

———. 1993. "Detecting the Scope of Rape: A Review of the Prevalence Research Methods." *Journal of Interpersonal Violence* 8:198-222.

Koss, Mary P., and T.E. Dinero. 1989. "A Discriminant Analysis of Risk Factors for Rape among a National Sample of College Women." *Journal of Consulting and Clinical Psychology* 57:242-50.

Koss, Mary P., C.A. Gidycz, and N. Wisniewski. 1987. "The Scope of Rape: Incidence and Prevalence of Sexual Aggression and Victimization in a National Sample of Higher Education Students." *Journal of Consulting and Clinical Psychology* 55:162-70.

Koss, Mary, and Lynette Heslet. 1992. "Somatic Consequences of Violence against Women." *Archives of Family Medicine* 1:53-59.

Koss, Mary, P. Koss, and J. Woodruff. 1991. "Deleterious Effects of Criminal Victimization on Women's Health and Medical Utilization." *Archives of Internal Medicine* 151:342-47.

Koss, Mary P., and C.J. Oros. 1982. "Sexual Experiences Survey: A Research Instrument Investigating Sexual Aggression and Victimization." *Journal of Consulting and Clinical Psychology* 50:455-57.

Kristof, Nicholas. 1993. "Chinese Turn to Ultrasound, Scorning Baby Girls for Boys." *New York Times,* July 27, p. A1.

LaPin, Deirde. 1992. "Assessing Psychosocial Needs of Refugee Women and Children Using Rapid Field Techniques." Paper presented at the 120th Annual Meeting of the American Public Health Association, Washington, D.C., November 8-12.

Larrain, Soledad. 1993. "Estudio de Frecuencia de la Violencia Intrafamiliar y la Condición de la Mujer en Chile." Pan-American Health Organization, Santiago, Chile.

Lentzner, H.R., and M.M. DeBerry. 1980. *Intimate Victims: A Study of Violence among Friends and Relatives.* Washington, D.C.: U.S. Department of Justice, Bureau of Justice Statistics.

Leslie, JoAnne. 1992. "Women's Lives and Women's Health: Using Social Science Research to Promote Better Health for Women." Paper commissioned as part of the joint program of the Population Council/International Center for Research on Women on Family Structure, Female Headship and Maintenance of Families in Poverty. Population Council, New York.

Levine, R.A., Sara E. Levine, Amy Richman, and Clara Sunderland Correa. 1987. "Schooling and Maternal Behavior in a Mexican City: The Effects on Fertility and Child Survival." Fertility Determinants Research Notes 16. Population Council, New York.

Levinson, David. 1988. "Family Violence in Cross-Cultural Perspective." In Vincent Van Hasselt and others, editors, *Handbook of Family Violence.* New York: Plenum Publishers.

———. 1989. *Violence in Cross-Cultural Perspective.* Newbury Park: Sage Publishers.

Lightfoot-Klein, Hanny. 1989. *Prisoners of Ritual.* Binghamton, N.Y.: Harrington Park Press.

Lindenbaum, Shirley, M. Chakraborty, and M. Elias. 1985. "The Influence of Maternal Education on Infant and Child Mortality in Bangladesh." Special Publication 23. International Centre for Diarrhoeal Disease Research, Dhaka, Bangladesh.

Liskin, L.S. 1981. "Periodic Abstinence: How Well Do New Approaches Work?" Population Reports. Johns Hopkins School of Hygiene and Public Health, Population Information Program, Baltimore, Md.

Lundgren, R., and others. 1992. "Guatemala City Women: Empowering a Hidden Risk Group to Prevent HIV Transmission." Final technical report, phase I. DataPro SA and the Association Guatemalteca para la Prevencion y Control del SIDA, Guatemala City.

Lupri, E. 1989. "Male Violence in the Home." *Canadian Social Trends* 14:19-21.

Mahajan, A. 1990. "Instigators of Wife Battering." In Sushma Sood, editor, *Violence Against Women.* Jaipur, India: Arihant Publishers.

Maher, Monica. 1993. Director, Project Concern's Women's Program of Uraco Pueblo, Uraco, Honduras. Personal communication.

Maiuro, R.D., and others. 1988. "Anger, Hostility, and Depression in Domestically Violent versus Generally Assaultive Men and Nonviolent Control Subjects." *Journal of Consulting and Clinical Psychology* 56(1):17-23.

Marcelo, A.B. 1992. "A Sharing of Thoughts and Perspectives on Women's Health." *Association of Women in Development Newsletter* 6(2):6-7.

"Maridos Secuestradores." 1992. *La Nación,* October 7.

Marshall, W.L., Robin Jones, Tony Ward, Peter Johnston, and H.E. Barbaree. 1990. "Treatment Outcome with Sex Offenders." *Clinical Psychology Review* 11(4):465.

MATCH International. 1990. *Linking Women's Global Struggles to End Violence.* Ottawa, Ontario: MATCH International Centre.

Mathur, Kanchan. 1992. "Bhateri Rape Case: Backlash and Protest." *Economic and Political Weekly,* October 10.

McCleer, S.V., and R. Anwar. 1989. "A Study of Women Presenting in an Emergency Department." *American Journal of Public Health* 79:65-67.

McFarlane, Judith, and others. 1992. "Assessing for Abuse during Pregnancy: Severity and Frequency of Injuries and Associated Entry Into Prenatal Care." *Journal of the American Medical Society* 267(23):3176-78.

Mercy, James, and Linda Saltzman. 1989. "Fatal Violence among Spouses in the United States, 1976-1985." *American Journal of Public Health* 79(5):595-99.

Miller, Brenda A. 1990. "The Interrelationships between Alcohol and Drugs and Family Violence." In Mario De La Rosa, Elizabeth Y. Lambert, and Bernard Gropper, editors, *Drugs and Violence: Causes, Correlates, and Consequences.* NIDA Research Monograph 103. Rockville, Md.: National Institute on Drug Abuse.

Miller, Brenda A., William Downs, and Maria Testa. Forthcoming. "Interrelationships between Victimization Experiences and Women's Alcohol/Drug Use." *Journal of Alcohol Studies.*

Miller, Brenda A., and others. 1987. "The Role of Childhood Sexual Assault in the Development of Alcoholism in Women." *Violence and Victims* 2:157-72.

Mohamud, Asha. 1991. "Medical and Cultural Aspects of Female Circumcision in Somalia and Recent Efforts for Eradication." Paper presented at the 18th Annual National Council of International Health (NCIH) International Health Conference, Arlington, Va., June.

Moore, Kristin Anderson, Christine Winquist Nord, and James Peterson. 1989. "Nonvoluntary Sexual Activity among Adolescents." *Family Planning Perspectives* 21(3):110-14.

Motsei, Mmatshilo. 1993. "Detection of Woman Battering in Health Care Settings: The Case of Alexandra Health Clinic." University of the Witwatersrand, Department of Community Health, The Centre for Health Policy, Johannesburg, South Africa.

Mullen, P.E., S.E. Romans-Clarkson, V.A. Walton, and P.E. Herbison. 1988. "Impact of Sexual and Physical Abuse on Women's Mental Health." *Lancet* 1:841.

Murray, Christopher. Forthcoming. "Quantifying the Burden of Disease: The Technical Basis for Disability Adjusted Life Years." *WHO Bulletin.*

Murray, Christopher, and Alan Lopez. Forthcoming. "Quantifying the Burden of Disability: Data, Methods and Results." *WHO Bulletin.*

Name withheld. 1992. "Violence against Women in China." Harvard University, Cambridge, Mass. Available from authors.

Nash, Nathaniel. 1992. "Bolivia Is Helping Its Battered Wives to Stand Up." *New York Times,* March 30.

National Committee for Injury Prevention and Control. 1989. *Injury Prevention: Meeting the Challenge.* New York: Oxford University Press.

NCVAW (National Committee on Violence Against Women). 1991. Pamphlet. Canberra, Australia: Office of the Status of Women.

Nevo, Jessica. 1993. "Femicide: The Social Construction of the Problem in Israel." Paper presented at the Fifth International Interdisciplinary Congress on Women, San Jose, Costa Rica, February.

Norris, Fran. 1992. "Epidemiology of Trauma, Frequency and Impact of Different Potentially Traumatic Events on Different Demographic Groups." *Journal of Consulting and Clinical Psychology* 60:409-18.

Ojeda, Adriana Perez, and Flor Draguicevic Perez. 1992. "Estudio Descriptivo y Analítico de Casos de Mujeres Agredidas entre los anos 1988-1989, registrados en el Hospital Regional y Juzgados de

Policia Local de Punta Arenas." *Mujer y Violenca Intrafamiliar*. Fundación Para El Desarrolo, Region XII, Magallanes, Chile.

OPS (Organizacion Panamericana de la Salud). 1992. *Violencia Contra La Mujer un Problema de Salud Publica: Memoria*. Managua, Nicaragua.

Paltiel, Freda. 1987. "Women and Mental Health: A Post Nairobi Perspective." *World Health Statistics Quarterly* 40:233-66.

Paone, Denise, and Wendy Chavkin. 1993. "From the Private Family Domain to the Public Health Forum: Sexual Abuse, Women and Risk for HIV Prevention." *SIECUS Report* 21(4).

Parker, Barbara, Judith McFarlane, Karen Soeken, Sarah Torres, and Doris Campbell. 1993. "Physical and Emotional Abuse in Pregnancy: A Comparison of Adult and Teenage Women." *Nursing Research* 42(3):173-78

Pawar, M.S. 1990. "Women and Family Violence: Policies and Programs." In Sushman Sood, editor, *Violence against Women*. Jaipur, India: Arihant Publishers.

Perez, Amelia Marquez. 1990. "Aproximación Diagnóstica a Las Violaciones de Mujeres en Los Distritos de Panamá y San Miguelito." Centro Para El Desarrollo de la Mujer, Universidad de Panamá, Panama City.

Perlez, Jane. 1991. "Kenyans Do Some Soul-Searching after the Rape of 71 Schoolgirls." *New York Times*, July 29.

Peters, S.D., G.E. Wyatt, and D. Finkelhor. 1986. "Prevalence." In D. Finkelhor, editor, *A Source Book on Child Sexual Abuse*. Beverly Hills: Sage Publications.

Phiri, Elizabeth. 1992. "Violence against Women in Zambia." Young Womens Christian Association, Lusaka.

Pitanguy, Jacqueline. 1993. Director, CEPIA (Citizenship, Studies, Information and Action). Personal communication. March 30.

Ponce, Alicia, Gladys Palan, and Alexandra Jacome. 1992. *Mujeres Latinoamericanas en Cifras: Ecuador*. Madrid: Ministerio de Asuntos Sociales, Instituto de la Mujer.

Popular Education Research Group. 1992. *Women Educating to End Violence against Women*. Toronto.

Population Council. 1991. "Summary of the Indonesian Epidemiology Network and the Population Council Workshop on Women's Health in Southeast Asia." New York.

Portugal, Ana Maria. 1988. "Crónica de una Violacion Provocada?" *Revista Mujer/Fempress*

"Contraviolencia.*" Santiago, Chile: FEMPRESS-ILET.

Post, Tom. 1993. "A Pattern of Rape." *Newsweek*, January 4.

Procurador de Justicia del Distrito Federal de Mexico. 1990. *Carpeta Basica*. Mexico City.

PROFAMILIA. 1990. *Encuestra de Prevalencia, Demografía y Salud*. Demographic and Health Survey. Bogatá.

———. 1992. *La Violencia y Los Derechos Humanos de la Mujer*. Bogata.

Querol, Mariano. 1992. Director of Mental Health, Ministry of Health, Peru. Personal communication. December 4.

Rachley, S.F. 1990. "An Investigation of Social Support and Sexual Abuse History in Victims of Childhood Sexual Abuse." Dissertation. Nova University, Fort Lauderdale, Florida. As cited in Mary Ann Dutton, *Empowering and Healing the Battered Woman*, New York: Springer Publishing Company, 1992.

Raikes, Alanagh. 1990. *Pregnancy, Birthing and Family Planning in Kenya: Changing Patterns of Behavior: A Health Utilization Study in Kissi District*. Copenhagen: Centre for Development Research.

Ramanamma, Hamid. 1990. "Female Foeticide and Infanticide: A Silent Violence." In Sushman Sood, editor, *Violence against Women*. Jaipur, India: Arihant Publishers.

Ramirez Rodriguez, Juan Carlos, and Griselda Uribe Vazquez. Forthcoming. "Mujer y violencia: un hecho cotidiano." *Salud Pública de Mexico* (Instituto Nacional de Salud Publica, Cuernavaca).

Rao, Vijayendra. 1993. Personal communication. Population Studies Center, University of Michigan, Ann Arbor.

Rao, Vijayendra, and Francis Bloch. 1993. "Wife-beating, Its Causes and Its Implication for Nutrition Allocations to Children: An Economic and Anthropological Case Study of A Rural South Indian Community." World Bank, Policy Research Department, Poverty and Human Resources Division, Washington, D.C. Draft.

Rao Gupta, Geeta. 1993. Personal communication. Institute for Research on Women, Washington, D.C., April.

Riley, I., D. Wohlfahrt, and E. Carrad. 1985. "The Management of Rape and Other Sexual Offenses in Port Moresby." Report of a workshop, Department of Community Medicine, University of Papua New Guinea, Port Moresby General Hospital, June 4.

Romkens, Renee. 1989. "Violence in Heterosexual Relationships: A National Research into the Scale,

Nature, Consequences and Backgrounds."
University of Amsterdam, Foundation for
Scientific Research on Sexuality and Violence.

"Rompiendo el Silencio." 1992. *La Boletina Managua*
(Puntos de Encuentro, Nicaragua) (9, Octo-
ber/November).

Rosas, M. Isabel. 1992. "Violencia Sexual y Política
Criminal." Comite Latinoamericano para la
Defensa de las Dereches de la Mujer (CLADEM)
Informativo 6. Lima, Peru.

Rosenberg, Tina. 1992. "Women and the Law in
Latin America: Machismo Still Prevails, But Not
without Challenge." Ford Foundation Report, New
York.

Rosenfeld, Barry. 1992. "Court-Ordered Treatment of
Spouse Abuse." *Clinical Psychology Review*
12:205-26.

Russell, D.E.H. 1983. "The Incidence and Prevalence
of Intrafamilial and Extrafamilial Sexual Abuse of
Female Children." *Child Abuse and Neglect* 7:133-
46.

———. 1986. *The Secret Trauma: Incest in the Lives
of Girls and Women.* New York: Basic Books.

Sacco, Vincent F., and Holly Johnson. 1990. *Patterns
of Criminal Victimization in Canada.* Ottawa:
Statistics Canada.

Sanday, Peggy Reeves. 1981. "The Socio-cultural
Context of Rape: A Cross-Cultural Study."
Journal of Social Issues 37(4):5-27.

Sapp, Allen, and Michael Vaughn. 1991. "Sex
Offender Rehabilitation Programs in State Prisons:
A Nationwide Survey." *Journal of Offender
Rehabilitation* 17(1/2):55-75.

Saunders, David, and Sandra Azar. 1989. "Treatment
Programs for Family Violence." In L. Ohlin and
M. Tonry, editors, *Family Violence.* Chicago:
University of Chicago Press.

Schei, Berit, and L.S. Bakketeig. 1989.
"Gynecological Impact of Sexual and Physical
Abuse by Spouse: A Study of a Random Sample of
Norwegian Women." *British Journal of Obstetrics
and Gynecology* 96:1379-83.

Schmidt, Janell, and Lawrence Sherman. 1993. "Does
Arrest Deter Domestic Violence?" *American
Behavioral Scientist* 36(5):601-09.

Schwartz, Martin D. 1987. "Gender and Injury in
Spousal Assault." *Sociological Focus* 20:61-75.

Sen, Amartya. 1990. "More than One Million Women
Are Missing." *New York Review of Books,*
December 20.

Servicio Nacional de la Mujer. 1991. *Perfil de la
Mujer: Argumentos Para un Cambio.* Santiago,
Chile.

Shamim, Ishrat. 1985. "Kidnapped, Raped, Killed:
Recent Trends in Bangladesh." Paper presented at
the International Conference on Families in the
Face of Urbanization, New Delhi, December 2-5.

Sheikh-Hashim, Leila, and Anna Gabba. 1990.
"Violence against Women in Dar es Salaam: A
Case Study of Three Districts." Tanzania Media
Women's Association, Dar es Salaam.

Sherman, Lawrence W., and Richard Berk. 1984.
"The Specific Deterrent Effects of Arrest for
Domestic Assault." *American Sociological Review*
49:261-71.

Sherman, Lawrence W., and Douglas Smith. 1992.
"Crime, Punishment and Stake in Conformity:
Legal and Informal Control of Domestic
Violence." *American Sociological Review* 57:680-
90.

Shim, J.K. 1988. "Family Violence and Aggression."
In K.I. Kim, editor, *Family Violence: The Fact
and Management.* Seoul: Tamgudang.

Shim, Young-Hee. 1992. "Sexual Violence against
Women in Korea: A Victimization Survey of Seoul
Women." Paper presented at conference on
International Perspectives: Crime, Justice and
Public Order, St. Petersburg, Russia, June 21-27.

Shrader Cox, Elizabeth, and Rosaria Valdez Santiago.
1992. "La violencia hacia la mujer Mexicana como
problema de salud pública: La incidencia de la
violencia doméstica en una microregion de Ciudad
Nexahualcoyotl." Centro de Investigación y Lucha
Contra la Violencia Doméstica (CECOVID),
Mexico City.

Skogan, W.G., and M.G. Maxfield. 1981. *Coping
with Crime: Victimization, Fear and Reactions to
Crime in Three American Cities.* Beverly Hills:
Sage Publications.

Smith, Michael. 1987. "The Incidence and Prevalence
of Woman Abuse in Toronto." *Violence and
Victims* 2:33-37.

Sogbetun, A.O., K.O. Alausa, and A.O. Osoba.
1977. "Sexually Transmitted Disease in Ibadan,
Nigeria." *British Journal of Venereal Disease*
53:158.

Sonali, Deraniyagala. 1990. "An Investigation into the
Incidence and Causes of Domestic Violence in Sri
Lanka." Women in Need (WIN), Colombo, Sri
Lanka.

Stark, Evan. 1984. "The Battering Syndrome: Social
Knowledge, Social Therapy and the Abuse of
Women." Ph.D dissertation, State University of
New York, Binghamton, Department of Sociology.

———. 1993. "In Defense of Mandatory Arrest: A
Reply to Its Critics." *American Behavioral
Scientist* 36(5):651-80.

Stark, Evan, and Anne Flitcraft. 1991. "Spouse Abuse." In Mark Rosenburg and Mary Ann Fenley, editors, *Violence in America: A Public Health Approach*. New York: Oxford University Press.

Stark, Evan, Anne Flitcraft, and W. Frazier. 1979. "Medicine and Patriarchal Violence: The Social Construction of a Private Event." *International Journal of Health Services* 9:461-93.

Stark, Evan, Anne Flitcraft, B. Zuckerman, A. Grey, J. Robinson, and W. Frazier. 1981. *Wife Abuse in the Medical Setting: An Introduction for Health Personnel*. Monograph 7. Washington, D.C.: Office of Domestic Violence.

Statistics Canada. 1990. "Conjugal Violence against Women." *Juristat* 10(7):1-7.

———. 1993. "The Violence against Women Survey." *The Daily: Statistics Canada,* November 18.

Steinman, M. 1989. "Lowering Recidivism among Men Who Batter Women." *Journal of Police Science and Administration* 17:124-32.

Stewart, Sheelagh. 1992. "Working the System: Sensitizing the Police to the Plight of Women." In Margaret Schuler, editor, *Freedom from Violence*. New York: UNIFEM.

Stops, Maria, and G. Larry Mays. 1991. "Treating Adolescent Sex Offenders in a Multi-Cultural Community Setting." *Journal of Offender Rehabilitation* 17(1/2):87-103.

Stordeur, Richard, and Richard Stille. 1989. *Ending Men's Violence against Their Partners: One Road to Peace*. Newbury Park, Cal.: Sage Publications.

Straus, M.A., and R.J. Gelles. 1986. "Societal Change and Change in Family Violence from 1975 to 1985 as Revealed by Two National Surveys." *Journal of Marriage and the Family* 48:465-79.

Swiss, Shana, and Joan Giller. 1993. "Rape as a Crime of War: A Medical Perspective." *Journal of the American Medical Association* 270(5):612-15.

Teske, Raymond, Jr., and Mary Parker. 1983. "Spouse Abuse in Texas: A Study of Women's Attitudes and Experiences." Department of Human Resources, Austin, Texas.

Toft, S., editor. 1986. *Domestic Violence in Papua New Guinea*. Law Reform Commission Occasional Paper 19. Port Morseby, Papua New Guinea.

Tolman, R.M., and L.W. Bennett. 1990. "A Review of Quantitative Research on Men Who Batter." *Journal of Interpersonal Violence* 5(1):87-118.

Toubia, Nahid. 1993. *Female Genital Mutilation: A Call for Global Action*. Available from Women, Ink. 777 United Nations Plaza, New York, New York.

Treguear, Tatiana L., and Carmen Carro. 1991. *Niñas Madres: Recuento de una Experiencia*. San Jose, Costa Rica: La Fundación Promoción, Capacitación y Accion Alternativa (PROCAL).

Ugalde, Juan Gerardo. 1988. "Sindrome de la Mujer Agredida." *Mujer* (Cefemina, San Jose, Costa Rica) 5.

UNICEF (United Nations Children's Fund). 1986. *Statistical Review of the Situation of Children of the World*. New York.

United Nations. 1989. *Violence against Women in the Family*. New York. Sales No. E.89.IV.5.

———. 1991. *The World's Women 1970-1990: Trends and Statistics*. Social Statistics and Indicators, Series K, No. 8. New York.

U.S. Congress. Senate. Judiciary Committee. 1990. "Ten Facts about Violence against Young Women." August 29. Washington, D.C.

Valdez, Teresa. 1992. *Mujeres Latinoamericanas en Cifras: Chile*. Madrid: Ministerio de Asuntos Sociales, Instituto de la Mujer.

van der Kolk, B.A. 1988. "The Trauma Spectrum: The Interaction of Biological and Social Events in the Genesis of the Trauma Response." *Journal of Traumatic Stress* 1(3):273-90.

Vargas Alvarado, E. 1983. *Medicina Legal*. San Jose: Lehmann Editores.

Vasquez, R., and G. Tamayo. 1989. *Violencia y Legalidad*. Lima: Concytec.

Vogelman, Lloyd, and Gillian Eagle. 1991. "Overcoming Endemic Violence against Women in South Africa." *Social Justice* 18(1-2):209-29.

Wakabi, Yeri, and Hope Mwesigye. 1991. "Violence against Women in Uganda: A Research Report." Association of Ugandan Women Lawyers (FIDA), Kampala.

Walker, Lenore. 1989. *Terrifying Love: Why Battered Women Kill and How Society Responds*. New York: Harper and Row.

Warsame, Mohamed. 1988. "Medical and Social Aspects of Female Circumcision in Somalia." In Somali Women's Democratic Organization, editor, *Female Circumcision: Strategies to Bring about Change*. Proceedings of the International Seminar on Female Circumcision, June 13-16.

Warshaw, C. 1989. "Limitations of the Medical Model in the Care of Battered Women." *Gender and Society* 3(4):506-17.

White, D.N., and others. 1989. *Treating Child Abuse and Family Violence in Hospitals*. Lexington, Mass.: Lexington Books.

WHO (World Health Organization). 1985. *World Health Statistics Annual*. Geneva.

"Wife Beating." 1987. *World Development Forum* (June 15).

Wilson-Brewer, Renee, Stu Cohen, Lydia O'Donnel, and Irene Goodman. 1991. *Violence Prevention for Young Adolescents: A Survey of the State of the Art.* Washington, D.C.: Carnegie Council on Adolescent Development.

Women's AID Organization. 1992. "Draft Report of the National Study on Domestic Violence." Kuala Lumpur, Malaysia.

Women's Legal Bureau. 1992. *A Primer on the SIBOL Rape Bill.* Quezon City, Philippines.

Women's World (ISIS-WICCE, Geneva). 1991-92. Volume 26, various issues.

World Bank. 1993. *World Development Report 1993: Investing in Health.* New York: Oxford University Press.

Worth, Dooley. 1989. "Sexual Decision-making and AIDS: Why Condom Promotion among Vulnerable Women Is Likely to Fail." *Studies in Family Planning* 20(6):297-307.

———. 1991. "Sexual Violence against Women and Substance Abuse." Working draft presented to the Domestic Violence Task Force, New York, January.

Wu Han. 1986. "United Nations Case Study of China." In *Proceedings of the Expert Group Meeting on Violence in the Family with a Special Emphasis on its Effects.* New York: United Nations, Division for the Advancement of Women.

Wyatt, Gail E. 1985. "The Sexual Abuse of Afro-American and White Women in Childhood." *Child Abuse and Neglect* 9:507-19.

———. 1988. "The Relationship between Child Sexual Abuse and Adolescent Sexual Functioning in Afro-American and White American Women." *Annals of the New York Academy of Sciences* 528:111-22.

Wyatt, Gail E., Donald Guthrie, and Cindy Notgrass. 1992. "The Differential Effects of Women's Child Sexual Abuse and Subsequent Sexual Revictimization." *Journal of Consulting and Clinical Psychology* 60(2):167-73.

Wyatt, Gail E., and G.J. Powell. 1988. *Lasting Effects of Child Sexual Abuse.* Newbury Park, Cal.: Sage Publications.

Zapata, B.C., A. Rebolledo, and E. Atalah. 1992. "The Influence of Social and Political Violence on the Risk of Pregnancy Complications." *American Journal of Public Health* 82(5):685-90.

Zeng Yi, Tu Ping, and Gu Baochang. 1993. "Causes and Implications of the Increase in China's Reported Sex Ratio at Birth." *Population and Development Review* 19(2):283-302.

Zierler, Sally, Lisa Feingold, Deborah Laufer, Priscilla Velentgas, Ira Kantrowitz-Gordon, and Kenneth Mayer. 1991. "Adult Survivors of Childhood Sexual Abuse and Subsequent Risk of HIV Infection." *American Journal of Public Health* 81(5):572-75.

Zurutuza, Cristina. 1993. "Domestic Violence: Strategies Used by the Latin American Women's Movement." In *Women Watched and Punished.* Lima: Comité Latinoamericano para la Defensa de las Dereches de la Mujer (CLADEM).

Distributors of World Bank Publications

ARGENTINA
Carlos Hirsch, SRL
Galeria Guemes
Florida 165, 4th Floor-Ofc. 453/465
1333 Buenos Aires

**AUSTRALIA, PAPUA NEW GUINEA,
FIJI, SOLOMON ISLANDS,
VANUATU, AND WESTERN SAMOA**
D.A. Information Services
648 Whitehorse Road
Mitcham 3132
Victoria

AUSTRIA
Gerold and Co.
Graben 31
A-1011 Wien

BANGLADESH
Micro Industries Development
   Assistance Society (MIDAS)
House 5, Road 16
Dhanmondi R/Area
Dhaka 1209

   Branch offices:
   Pine View, 1st Floor
   100 Agrabad Commercial Area
   Chittagong 4100

BELGIUM
Jean De Lannoy
Av. du Roi 202
1060 Brussels

CANADA
Le Diffuseur
151A Boul. de Mortagne
Boucherville, Québec
J4B 5E6

Renouf Publishing Co.
1294 Algoma Road
Ottawa, Ontario
K1B 3W8

CHILE
Invertec IGT S.A.
Av. Santa Maria 6400
Edificio INTEC, Of. 201
Santiago

CHINA
China Financial & Economic
   Publishing House
8, Da Fo Si Dong Jie
Beijing

COLOMBIA
Infoenlace Ltda.
Apartado Aereo 34270
Bogota D.E.

COTE D'IVOIRE
Centre d'Edition et de Diffusion
   Africaines (CEDA)
04 B.P. 541
Abidjan 04 Plateau

CYPRUS
Center of Applied Research
Cyprus College
6, Diogenes Street, Engomi
P.O. Box 2006
Nicosia

DENMARK
SamfundsLitteratur
Rosenoerns Allé 11
DK-1970 Frederiksberg C

DOMINICAN REPUBLIC
Editora Taller, C. por A.
Restauración e Isabel la Católica 309
Apartado de Correos 2190 Z-1
Santo Domingo

EGYPT, ARAB REPUBLIC OF
Al Ahram
Al Galaa Street
Cairo

The Middle East Observer
41, Sherif Street
Cairo

FINLAND
Akateeminen Kirjakauppa
P.O. Box 128
SF-00101 Helsinki 10

FRANCE
World Bank Publications
66, avenue d'Iéna
75116 Paris

GERMANY
UNO-Verlag
Poppelsdorfer Allee 55
D-5300 Bonn 1

HONG KONG, MACAO
Asia 2000 Ltd.
46-48 Wyndham Street
Winning Centre
2nd Floor
Central Hong Kong

HUNGARY
Foundation for Market Economy
Dombovari Ut 17-19
H-1117 Budapest

INDIA
Allied Publishers Private Ltd.
751 Mount Road
Madras - 600 002

   Branch offices:
   15 J.N. Heredia Marg
   Ballard Estate
   Bombay - 400 038

   13/14 Asaf Ali Road
   New Delhi - 110 002

   17 Chittaranjan Avenue
   Calcutta - 700 072

   Jayadeva Hostel Building
   5th Main Road, Gandhinagar
   Bangalore - 560 009

   3-5-1129 Kachiguda
      Cross Road
   Hyderabad - 500 027

   Prarthana Flats, 2nd Floor
   Near Thakore Baug, Navrangpura
   Ahmedabad - 380 009

   Patiala House
   16-A Ashok Marg
   Lucknow - 226 001

   Central Bazaar Road
   60 Bajaj Nagar
   Nagpur 440 010

INDONESIA
Pt. Indira Limited
Jalan Borobudur 20
P.O. Box 181
Jakarta 10320

IRAN
Kowkab Publishers
P.O. Box 19575-511
Tehran

IRELAND
Government Supplies Agency
4-5 Harcourt Road
Dublin 2

ISRAEL
Yozmot Literature Ltd.
P.O. Box 56055
Tel Aviv 61560

ITALY
Licosa Commissionaria Sansoni SPA
Via Duca Di Calabria, 1/1
Casella Postale 552
50125 Firenze

JAPAN
Eastern Book Service
Hongo 3-Chome, Bunkyo-ku 113
Tokyo

KENYA
Africa Book Service (E.A.) Ltd.
Quaran House, Mfangano Street
P.O. Box 45245
Nairobi

KOREA, REPUBLIC OF
Pan Korea Book Corporation
P.O. Box 101, Kwangwhamun
Seoul

Korean Stock Book Centre
P.O. Box 34
Yeoeido
Seoul

MALAYSIA
University of Malaya Cooperative
   Bookshop, Limited
P.O. Box 1127, Jalan Pantai Baru
59700 Kuala Lumpur

MEXICO
INFOTEC
Apartado Postal 22-860
14060 Tlalpan, Mexico D.F.

NETHERLANDS
De Lindeboom/InOr-Publikaties
P.O. Box 202
7480 AE Haaksbergen

NEW ZEALAND
EBSCO NZ Ltd.
Private Mail Bag 99914
New Market
Auckland

NIGERIA
University Press Limited
Three Crowns Building Jericho
Private Mail Bag 5095
Ibadan

NORWAY
Narvesen Information Center
Book Department
P.O. Box 6125 Etterstad
N-0602 Oslo 6

PAKISTAN
Mirza Book Agency
65, Shahrah-e-Quaid-e-Azam
P.O. Box No. 729
Lahore 54000

PERU
Editorial Desarrollo SA
Apartado 3824
Lima 1

PHILIPPINES
International Book Center
Suite 1703, Cityland 10
Condominium Tower 1
Ayala Avenue, H.V. dela
   Costa Extension
Makati, Metro Manila

POLAND
International Publishing Service
Ul. Piekna 31/37
00-677 Warzawa

For subscription orders:
IPS Journals
Ul. Okrezna 3
02-916 Warszawa

PORTUGAL
Livraria Portugal
Rua Do Carmo 70-74
1200 Lisbon

SAUDI ARABIA, QATAR
Jarir Book Store
P.O. Box 3196
Riyadh 11471

**SINGAPORE, TAIWAN,
MYANMAR,BRUNEI**
Gower Asia Pacific Pte Ltd.
Golden Wheel Building
41, Kallang Pudding, #04-03
Singapore 1334

SOUTH AFRICA, BOTSWANA
For single titles:
Oxford University Press
   Southern Africa
P.O. Box 1141
Cape Town 8000

For subscription orders:
International Subscription Service
P.O. Box 41095
Craighall
Johannesburg 2024

SPAIN
Mundi-Prensa Libros, S.A.
Castello 37
28001 Madrid

Librería Internacional AEDOS
Consell de Cent, 391
08009 Barcelona

SRI LANKA AND THE MALDIVES
Lake House Bookshop
P.O. Box 244
100, Sir Chittampalam A.
   Gardiner Mawatha
Colombo 2

SWEDEN
For single titles:
Fritzes Fackboksforetaget
Regeringsgatan 12, Box 16356
S-103 27 Stockholm

For subscription orders:
Wennergren-Williams AB
P. O. Box 1305
S-171 25 Solna

SWITZERLAND
For single titles:
Librairie Payot
Case postale 3212
CH 1002 Lausanne

For subscription orders:
Librairie Payot
Service des Abonnements
Case postale 3312
CH 1002 Lausanne

THAILAND
Central Department Store
306 Silom Road
Bangkok

**TRINIDAD & TOBAGO, ANTIGUA
BARBUDA, BARBADOS,
DOMINICA, GRENADA, GUYANA,
JAMAICA, MONTSERRAT, ST.
KITTS & NEVIS, ST. LUCIA,
ST. VINCENT & GRENADINES**
Systematics Studies Unit
#9 Watts Street
Curepe
Trinidad, West Indies

UNITED KINGDOM
Microinfo Ltd.
P.O. Box 3
Alton, Hampshire GU34 2PG
England